Conversations
on the Character
of Princeton

Conversations on the Character of Princeton

By WILLIAM McCLEERY

PRINCETON UNIVERSITY
PRINCETON, NEW JERSEY

Published by Princeton University, Office of Communications/Publications
First printing—1986
Second printing—1986
Third printing (revised edition)—1990

Printed in the United States of America by Princeton University Press

Set in type by Elizabeth Typesetting Company and
the Office of University Printing Services

Designed by Mahlon L. Lovett
Cover drawing by Gillett Good Griffin

To order additional copies, write or call—
Office of Communications/Publications
Stanhope Hall, Princeton University, Princeton, New Jersey 08544-5264
609-258-3600

Contents

Introduction

LEWIS THOMAS

I don't know how many of the graduates of Princeton are beset, as I am from time to time, by guilty feelings for having gotten less than they might have from having studied in that great, dear place. I would guess that the number is large, maybe the majority that it should be if all were honest with themselves. For there is, and always was, more there to be taken away than even the more absorptive minds could possibly carry.

My father (1899) told me that I (1933) was lucky, luckier than he and his brothers Lew (1898) and Tom (1903). I could have, he said, a *modern* education. He had learned only the things that were known just before the turn of the century, an education in ignorance he called it, while I had before me all the vast store of knowledge accumulated during the first third of the twentieth century, and now I could get at it. It would be up to me.

He took for granted, as I came to do, that Princeton was a place designed primarily, maybe solely, for learning. He envied me the preceptorial system, which had come in after his time, and wished he had that experience, but even without it his memories were filled with the teachers he had known for the four years between 1895 and 1899; his one regret was that he had learned less than he could have if only he'd kept his socks pulled

Lewis Thomas, M.D., Princeton Class of 1933, is president emeritus of Memorial Sloan-Kettering Cancer Center and author of the prize-winning books *The Lives of a Cell* and *The Medusa and the Snail*. He has been on the medical school faculties of Cornell, New York University, Rockefeller University, and Yale.

up and tried harder. When he talked of this, about how much Princeton had offered him and how much less he had been able to take, he sounded wistful. If he had it to do over, he said, and eyed me with purpose.

It is like this for me, looking back more than a half century. I had no idea at the time, back in the thirties, that the university was unique. I took it as simply given that the faculty were there as my friends, almost an extension of my family, ready to explore life itself in any complexity with me tagging along as a younger cousin, yelping in curiosity, everyone perplexed together. I could, I discovered, take it or leave it. I took some, enough to get on with, and left some. Ever since, I've wished I'd had more sense and taken it all, or anyway more than I did.

The term "research university" had not yet been invented, but it was plain that a lot of people on the faculty were devoted to research, and it never crossed anyone's mind that this endeavor was secondary to, or interfered with, the teaching of undergraduates. Indeed, as I recall, *teaching* was not the word to describe what went on, *learning* was.

The pages of this book are testimony that Princeton has not changed. In the face of a spectacular expansion of her research and graduate education programs, the undergraduate students remain, as always, at the center of the university's concern. Best of all, the faculty take vast pleasure in this concern, they take pride in the quality of their undergraduate teaching, they even appear, for all the seriousness of this intensely serious institution, to be having the greatest fun.

Foreword

HAROLD T. SHAPIRO

W hen the decision was made to bring out this new edition of *Conversations* (first published in 1986), it seemed appropriate to lead it off with some words from an educator who had spent much of the last two years intensively studying Princeton's character in his role as its new president.

Harold T. Shapiro readily agreed to sit for a conversational foreword, saying he had read the book while first considering the Princeton presidency, it had contributed to his understanding of the University, and he would be glad to talk about it and about his own view of Princeton's character.

Our conversation took place in his large Nassau Hall office looking out on Cannon Green, he in shirt sleeves seated behind his desk, looking young for his 55 years, and eager to get to the subjects at hand.

Speaking first of the book, he called it "a self-portrait of Princeton at one point in its recent history. It has changed some since the conversations took place, but not in the fundamental principles set forth. The book is to some extent an idealization, but we still subscribe to the ideals. Some of the persons who appear are no longer with us, but

---

Harold T. Shapiro—A.B. McGill University, Ph.D. Princeton (1964)—became Princeton's 18th president in January 1988 after eight years as president of the University of Michigan. He is also a professor of economics as he was at Michigan. He is a member of the Institute of Medicine, the Conference Board Inc., the New Jersey Commission on Science and Technology, and the Government-University-Industry Research Roundtable of the National Academy of Sciences. A trustee of the Alfred P. Sloan Foundation, the Interlochen Center for the Arts, and the Universities Research Association, he serves as a director of the American Council on Education, the Dow Chemical Company, and the National Bureau of Economic Research.

I believe they still fairly represent today's faculty and administration and, I hope, tomorrow's. Anyone reading their remarks will gain useful insight into Princeton—and into education generally—and will get acquainted with some educators well worth knowing."

Turning to Princeton, he said he obviously could not come up with a significant characteristic that no one else had mentioned, "but the more I study the place, the more I find some of its basic characteristics combining to form an institution that, in many ways, seems to symbolize American education.

"The look of Princeton—its historic buildings and lovely campus—backed by its worldwide reputation for scholarship and research, and its dedication to the teaching of undergraduates—all of this seems to stand for, seems to *say*, 'education.'

"Princeton of course is not alone in having a symbolic quality. There are other institutions that have a grasp on the educational psyche of the country. But because of its uncommonly small size for an institution of such eminence, the symbolism is especially concentrated here."

He said the notion of Princeton as symbol had first struck him when he returned to the campus in 1987 to discuss the presidency (which he assumed in 1988), after being away since his days as a graduate student (1961–64).

"My old friends told me I wouldn't recognize the place, it had changed so much. The wonderful thing was, it felt just the same! New buildings had gone up, but in such a way that the old ones still dominated. There were changes around the edges but not at the center. I felt I had come back home. It had the impact of an environment I very clearly remembered. As Neil Rudenstine puts it (chapter 18), Princeton has a 'presence.' It doesn't leave you neutral. This presence is felt not just by Princetonians; even casual visitors to the campus seem affected by it.

"Partly because we're aware of Princeton's symbolism, I think most of us who work or have worked here, as students, faculty, or administrators, consider ourselves lucky—and duty-bound to do what we can in this generation to make sure that succeeding generations will have the same opportunities, and the same passion for the place, that we have. And this attitude is a significant element in Princeton's character, as it is in the character of any institution that arouses loyalty in its people."

Princeton's historic emphasis on serving the nation is a characteristic Shapiro considers major, and one he greatly admires. "Universities, public or private, have a broad public purpose: they exist to serve the country. Educate people, yes; produce new knowledge, yes; but in doing these things also provide leadership in various aspects of national life. That doesn't mean we should tell New York City whether to centralize its school system, or General Motors how many divisions it should have. We can't deal directly with substance abuse or air pollution or toxic wastes. We're not quick thinkers, we're deep thinkers. We can't give instantaneous advice; we're for careful and reflective thought. But people do look to us for help—and leadership—in dealing with whatever is bothering them. Most of what we discover does, eventually, contribute to solving down-to-earth problems, even though we don't always address them directly. There are institutions that do, and should, respond quickly. We're not one of them. But we should, and do, think deeply about things that matter.

"By being what we are, we draw talents upward and maximize those talents, and humankind is bound to benefit."

He said Princeton's status as a symbol placed a special responsibility on it to offer leadership.

In any special area today?

"In many areas. But since this book will be read mainly by students and teachers, let me say I think it's important for all institutions of higher learning to demonstrate more commitment to elementary and secondary education, which is now undergoing a major crisis in this country."

As for what Princeton can do, and is doing, to help, he said, "We have to be careful not to over-promise; but our scholars are exploring how people learn to learn, how they learn to *think*. Our faculty conduct special summer programs for teachers from surrounding communities. Every year at Commencement we pay symbolic tribute to secondary education by giving only one set of awards, other than degrees, and those are to outstanding teachers in New Jersey secondary schools. We encourage our students to consider teaching as a career through our Teacher Preparation Program.

"There may be other special programs we ought to develop, but, in the end, we help most by being what we are: an institution that puts a very high premium on teaching. Students work here under talented, dedicated, caring professors—the conversations in this book make this very clear. I don't see how any teacher, from kindergarten through college, could read these conversations without having his or her spirits lifted by discovering how scholars at the peak of their professions still feel about the art of teaching.

"Another way Princeton stands as a valuable symbol is by having kept its focus on the arts and sciences, even while giving serious attention to professional education in engineering, in architecture, and— at the Woodrow Wilson School—in public and international affairs. It's almost uncanny how Princeton has these strengths at a time when many students elsewhere have fled the arts and sciences—particularly the humanities—and when there is an extraordinary need in the country for broadly trained talent in engineering and public affairs.

"Finally, Princeton's steadfast commitment to undergraduate education when other research universities were concentrating on their graduate schools gives it a special timeliness today, because undergraduate education is where the greatest challenge in higher education is coming, where the most creativity and leadership will be required."

As he walked me out into the hall, he said it was surprising that Princeton's presence had made so deep an impression on him in his graduate school days since, during that earlier stay, "I didn't get inside more than three buildings!—Firestone Library, where my classes were; the Chancellor Green Center, where I often had lunch; and the dining hall at the Graduate College, where friends sometimes took me to dinner. I lived off campus with my wife and three children. It's a characteristic of Princeton that if you work hard, you can get a graduate degree in three years." He smiled. "I worked hard!"

While he declined to draw any invidious comparison with the University of Michigan, of which he was president before returning to Princeton, he did allow that because Princeton is so much smaller, "there are far fewer administrators between the president and both the students and the faculty—and that's a characteristic I like very much." He said that despite problems in American secondary schools "our students are coming in better educated than ever before, incredibly accomplished. They represent a treasure coequal to the faculty."

He called Princeton "a small, personal, and one-on-one community. You can feel the place vibrate with excitement. Alumni and visitors know it on special occasions— reunions, athletic events, performances, and exhibits at the Art Museum. I wish they could see students as we do, passing them on campus between classes, or meeting with them in class. I think you get a better sense of them from watching the teams practice than from seeing them play!"

—W. McC.

Preface

WILLIAM McCLEERY

Much as they have in common, all universities are different, and this anthology of informal conversations is intended to shed light on how Princeton is different—not just superficially, in personality and style, but fundamentally different: What distinctive traits give Princeton its *character*?

That was the question I took, in various forms, to more than forty Princeton scholars and administrators—and one coach—recommended to me as being extremely knowledgeable about Princeton and unusually qualified to compare it with other universities, particularly but not exclusively those of the Ivy League. Being by choice associated with Princeton, they obviously had some favorable bias toward it. But they also knew and cared about universities generally, and had reputations for objectivity and probity—and far better things to do with their time than sit around paying Princeton easy compliments.

They understood that I wanted testimony, not testimonials.

My hope was that their educated impressions would define Princeton more clearly for its present faculty, students, administrators, alumni, and friends, and would be of practical help to scholars and administrators considering joining the Princeton family, and

---

William McCleery—A.B. Nebraska—has been a reporter in the Associated Press Washington bureau, executive editor of the AP Feature Service, Sunday editor of *PM*, associate editor of the *Ladies Home Journal*, and editor of *University: A Princeton Quarterly*. Author of ten professionally produced plays (two on Broadway), he taught playwriting for twelve years at Princeton. He edited the public papers of Robert F. Goheen '40 into the book *The Human Nature of a University*.

to prospective students and their parents and guidance counselors. That remains this book's principal aim.

But as the conversations proceeded I came to believe that they might interest a broader audience as well; that much of what was being said about learning and teaching was applicable to other human organizations, including secondary schools, businesses, governments, churches, even families.

Some of those I talked with were reluctant at first to compare Princeton with other universities. But this seemed to me a good way to get at Princeton's character, and I supported my argument with some lines from Samuel Johnson's 1765 *Preface to Shakespeare:*

> As among the works of Nature no man can properly call a river deep, or a mountain high, without the knowledge of many mountains, and many rivers: so in the productions of genius, nothing can be styled excellent till it has been compared with other works of the same kind.

To minimize repetition and achieve an anthology of manageable length, my forty-some conversations have been reduced—with a good deal of personal pain and professional advice—to the twenty-five that appear here. My warm thanks to those who talked with me and deepened my understanding of Princeton—and of learning and teaching—but whose remarks do not appear.

Some repetition remains. Any institution has a limited number of genuinely character-determining traits, so it is not surprising that some of Princeton's are alluded to more than once. But each allusion, I think, casts a different light, colored by the personality and perceptiveness of the alluder. However many times the senior thesis had been mentioned before, how could one omit Carl Schorske's characterization of it?

The chapters are arranged alphabetically because that seemed a practical, even-handed method, but they need not be read in that order—though Carlos Baker *does* get right to the heart of Princeton's differentness even as William Bowen then delimits the number of traits that combine to form a university's character, and Theodore Ziolkowski wraps it all up with a fine philosophical flourish.

The material in the conversations might have been presented differently to make a quite different book, with chapter headings such as "Relations between Faculty and Students" and "Woodrow Wilson's Influence." But this would have deprived the reader of the pleasure of sitting down and conversing vicariously with some articulate, often witty human beings whose association with and enthusiasm for Princeton may say as much about the place as their words do.

Some readers may feel there is too little criticism here, but in fact many of the positive statements about Princeton have their negative connotations. "Princeton is small for a major university, and set in a small town" may be taken as praise by some, but not by those who want a large university in a large city. "The faculty is close to the students"—but not all students and certainly not all professors consider that a blessing.

The simple truth is, Princeton is a certain kind of place. The people quoted here make pretty clear *what* kind. Because they like it, their comments generally sound favorable. People who disliked it might have made much the same points, but would have colored them differently—and with less perceptiveness if one accepts the principle that we only truly understand what we love. This book does not attempt to touch on Princeton's every fault or every virtue, for many of both she shares with similar universities, and the aim here was an exposition of Princeton's differentness, not her every characteristic.

It may strike the reader that an anthology like this could be assembled about any university, with some of its own professors and administrators dwelling on its distinguishing traits. I agree—and believe we would all be the wiser for them. Each would add to our understanding of education the way a good biography of one however atypical human being sheds light on all human nature.

As Woodrow Wilson said in June 1907 to a gathering at Harvard on the occasion of his receiving, as president of Princeton, an honorary Harvard degree:

> Princeton is not like Harvard, and she does not wish to be. Neither does she wish Harvard to be like Princeton. She believes, as every thoughtful man must believe, that the strength of a democracy is in its variety, and that where there are a great many competing ideals,...the best ideal will survive the competition.... Now we at Princeton are in the arena and you at Harvard are in the arena; and, though ideals in the field of mind are not ideals in the field of politics, while it is not necessary that one should go down and the other survive, I do believe that every ideal flourishes by reason of the opposition made to it.

"You want to project not your own superior knowledge but your enthusiasm for the material, for finding...the buried notions beneath the lines."

1

CARLOS BAKER

I n the mid-1930s young Carlos Baker, A.M., was teaching at a preparatory school in Buffalo, New York. Already decided on scholarship as a career, he was pondering where to go for his Ph.D. in English when his headmaster, a Princeton alumnus, having sized him up, said, "Go to Princeton: you'll get to know your professors."

He took the advice and it turned out to be sound. As a graduate student, Baker so enjoyed Princeton that he stayed on for forty years as a member of the faculty. "This *is* a place where students and faculty get to know each other, and if I had to choose the one aspect of Princeton that most clearly distinguishes it, that would be it: The way the learners and teachers relate to each other.

"The same relationship exists at many excellent colleges. My own alma mater, Dartmouth, is similarly devoted to undergraduate teaching. But Princeton is a *university* and its faculty has access to graduate students and research facilities. There are, of course, other universities where individual scholars and scientists are

Widely known as essayist, critic, editor, and biographer *(Ernest Hemingway: A Life Story)*, Baker has also published novels, short stories, and poems. His most recent published works include *Ernest Hemingway: Selected Letters 1917–1961* and *The Echoing Green*, a study of poetry. He taught English at Princeton for forty years and was twice chairman of that department before retiring in 1977. He has a Dartmouth A.B., Harvard A.M., and Princeton Ph.D.

1

dedicated to teaching undergraduates, but those individuals tend to be exceptions. The concept of scholar-teacher is better realized here than at any other place I know of. There is less of the huffy standoffishness on the part of professors who'd like it known that what they say is The Truth; is not to be questioned; who regard the student as 'an ear attached to a digestive system.' To me, after four decades, Princeton seems more modest."

Now retired, Baker guest-lectured at many universities during his teaching years. "I was always glad to get back to Princeton—not only because the relationship between faculty and students was different but because, as a consequence, the quality of the students was different."

Different how?

He combed a sun-tanned hand through his thick white crewcut. "More reachable; more demanding, in a good way. Having been treated with a kind of respect that acknowledges their humanness, Princeton students seem less awed by their professors. This makes possible a kind of dialogue between the two that can't go on when the gap between them is too wide.

"Not all students and professors like, or function best in, this kind of dialogic relationship; there are those who prefer to distance themselves—and some do so even here. Most students, however, can learn more from someone they feel they know, who treats them as individuals and seems to care about them. But this caring is a matter of degree; a graded, graduated thing; not sentimental, though feelings enter in. You might call the relationship 'familial' *if* you acknowledge that parents have to exercise authority and take responsibility: I don't like the idea of professors getting palsy-walsy with their students. You might say at Princeton the student is a temporarily adopted child—in an intellectual sense."

Because of the Princeton faculty's accessibility, "students frequently acquire an unusual attitude toward learning: Some of their professors' enthusiasm for the material rubs off on them. They discover learning can be fun—*serious* fun, but fun. And they get enthusiastic about the give-and-take of teaching and learning. A kind of union develops between professor and students, a sense of common purpose.

"I don't say this goes on at no other university or invariably goes on at Princeton; but it's institutional and traditional here, and the high ratio of faculty to students makes it physically possible."

Does Princeton sacrifice something to get this relationship between faculty and students? He nodded.

"Some outstanding scholars leave, or decline to come, because they want more nonteaching hours to do what they regard as their 'own' work. They go elsewhere and attract graduate students we'd like to have. Luckily other great scholars enjoy relating to undergraduates."

There is, he conceded, conflict between teaching and scholarship. "When you're deep in teaching, your scholarship is bound to suffer some. But Princeton is more determined than most places to provide leaves for its faculty; by putting together leaves and summers you can get a good chunk of time for scholarship." Working this way it took him seven years to write his biography of Hemingway and another two and a half years to assemble and edit the Hemingway letters.

Good teaching is fostered at Princeton, he said, by the "preceptorial" system introduced by President Woodrow Wilson in 1905: One faculty member working with a small number of students to discuss material covered in lectures or assigned reading. "That was one of Wilson's greatest contributions. In somewhat modified form it still goes on. Lecturing is considered more prestigious, but I always found 'precepting' more fun.

"It's good teacher training because you can *see the*

reaction of students to the material. In fifty minutes you
can reach an extraordinarily high level of excitement and
intellectual joy. But it takes skill. You learn—you teach
yourself, and your students teach you—to keep it on
track, and yet spontaneous and exciting.

"Not all preceptorial sessions attain this level. Sometimes the students sit around like logs, depending on
the material—and the time of year! But when it's good
there's nothing like it. Lecturing, for me, never produced the same intellectual excitement.

"Precepting rarely goes on at its highest level for the
entire fifty minutes; and it doesn't happen early in a
course; you have to get to know your students. I always
got on a first-name basis with mine—before that was
the fashion—got to know their characteristics. You can
do this, given a small group; get a degree of familiarity
that's a necessary groundwork. You get them coming
forth quite soon, in the third or fourth session, if you
establish friendliness, what I call 'associationism,'
which is the basis for really good exchanges.

"You see one student getting excited about the material and you pull him along—'That's a good idea! Let's
kick it around!' —to stimulate general participation.
You say to a nonparticipant, 'Joe, can you add anything
to that?' A 'star' student can help you teach. But if you
let one student talk too much, you may lose the others.
You try to get at the center of an assignment while
working the edges as well.

"You have to guide—and push—without seeming to;
stay on top of the material *and* of the students, who
sometimes surprise you with their understanding and
sometimes with their almost total lack of it.

"You're out to sell the material, but you don't want to
seem overprepared. You want to project not your own
superior knowledge but your enthusiasm for the material, for finding its deeper meanings, the buried notions
beneath the lines. You have to come across as the leader

and yet convey a sense of codiscovery. You can't pretend you're coming on new truths at the same rate they are. But in the course of eliciting from them—and 'elicit' is the key word—you do learn things yourself. You have to be aggressive—keep introducing new ideas to encourage them to have ideas of their own—and yet modest, in the sense that you can't be dictatorial about what the material should mean to them. At one extreme, monologue; at the other, bull session. You need a genuine feeling that you, too, have something to learn."

Summing up, he said, "This may sound banal, but it's true: Under the guidance of good teachers, Princeton students do educate themselves. The excitement of *arriving at* truth—that's what learning is all about."

In contrast to—?

"To having it thrust upon you." He sighed.

"I can still see the faces of students in precepts, of one young woman in particular. We were discussing a poem by Wallace Stevens, reading it aloud. Suddenly dawn spread across her face like Aurora! Pink and rosy! 'Oh! I *see!*' The sense of discovery! Columbus couldn't have looked more excited and pleased when he first spotted America. That came-the-dawn effect is rare, but for a teacher it's one of the real rewards."

"It's the combination of characteristics, as much as the characteristics themselves, that defines an institution or a person; the way the different components act on each other."

2

WILLIAM G. BOWEN

As president of Princeton for more than a decade he must have gained unusual insight into how his university works, and how others work. Had this experience given him a new appreciation of how Princeton differs from others?

William Bowen was shaking his head. No?

"No," he said, "not a *new* appreciation. What I see today as Princeton's most significant characteristics I saw when I came here nearly thirty years ago as a graduate student. They were why I came."

What were those characteristics?

"Princeton seemed to me to combine two fundamental elements: one, outstanding academic quality, especially in my own field of labor economics, in which Princeton ranked as one of the leading universities in the world, and still does; and, two, a human scale that

Before becoming its seventeenth president in June 1972, Bowen—A.B. Denison, Ph.D. Princeton—served Princeton as an economics professor (he was appointed a full professor at age thirty-one, a record at that time) and as provost for the final five years of Robert F. Goheen's presidency. His books include *The Wage-Price Issue—A Theoretical Analysis;* (with Professor W. J. Baumol) *Performing Arts: The Economic Dilemma;* and (with T. A. Finegan) *The Economics of Labor Force Participation.* He has been chairman of the board of the Center for Advanced Study in the Behavioral Sciences, and is a regent of the Smithsonian Institution, a director of NCR Corporation, and a director of the Reader's Digest Association.

appealed to me. This combination still seems to me what is really special about Princeton. Not just one or the other, but the combination.

"I have, of course, become aware of institutional differences—in administration and structure—as a result of my experiences in this office." Including differences in the way decisions are made? "Yes. But these differences are not what I would call basic characteristics. They are means, not ends. They reflect Princeton's character, and support it, but they don't shape it as do the teaching and scholarship that occur here."

He paused.

"There *are* two other characteristics of Princeton that I've become more conscious of since my graduate student days and which I think are basic. One is the setting. Some of the learning that takes place here is a consequence of the physical beauty of the place, and its—at times!—tranquillity.

"The other element I now see more clearly as affecting Princeton's character is its history, by which I mean not only its tradition of academic quality but its commitment to service. This university simply wouldn't be what it is, or work as it does, if its history were different.

"So Princeton is the product of an intimate intertwining of several elements: of the way both undergraduate and graduate students are taught—by a single faculty of scholars doing serious research; in a relatively small place; of a certain beauty and atmosphere; and with a pervasive history. These elements cohere to a quite extraordinary degree and give the university a coherence I'm much more conscious of now than I was before becoming president."

By "coherence" he meant—?

"Most faculty members here see themselves as having responsibilities to the university as a whole. This is true to a greater extent at Princeton, I believe, than at comparable universities. And it's not only the faculty. The students, alumni, and staff seem to feel an affinity for the entire university, not just for their own part of it.

"Obviously, other places have each of the characteristics I've mentioned, but not in the same combination. And it's the combination of characteristics, as much as the characteristics themselves, that defines an institution or a person; the way the different components act on each other. To return to your question about decision making at Princeton—our pattern involves extensive participation, which wouldn't be possible without the cohesiveness; and the wide participation reinforces the cohesiveness."

Is Princeton's decision-making pattern unique, then?

"Let's say it's at one end of a scale."

At the other end of which would be what? Dictatorship?

He laughed and said he would prefer a more moderate term.

Is the president's job at Princeton very different from that at other universities of its caliber?

"Yes. Each presidency is different from the others, and Princeton's probably more so."

Different how?

"The president here is unusually fortunate in that the scale of the place allows a degree of intimate involvement with the essential business of a university—education and research—that isn't possible generally. I get a great deal of comfort and encouragement and pleasure, for example, from my teaching [in an introductory economics course] and from writing letters of recommendation for students I've had in my classes. It's a refreshing change from the administrative detail any president has to handle. I also enjoy the direct contact with faculty members, some of whom I came to know when they were deciding whether to come to Princeton. And as chairman of the Faculty's Advisory Committee on Appointments and Advancements, I have an opportunity to examine closely the health of each department.

"Hardly a day passes, when I'm here and not 'on the road,' that someone doesn't just drop in, from a student to a faculty member to a trustee passing through or a person from the town. There is an assumption of accessibility here that's unknown at more complex places. It's a desirable characteristic. While I'm not able to satisfy all the expectations created, I'm glad they're there, and I do my best."

So the Princeton presidency probably attracts a different kind of person?

"Well, anyone who doesn't like myriad roles would be unhappy in this office. I know personally the coaches of many teams, for example. It's something I happen to enjoy, but it is expected here. Princeton alumni expect the president to attend all sorts of gatherings, and I do a great deal of that. Major donors to this university generally expect to deal with the president. And that, too, is possible—and fine and healthy—here."

Does the character of the university shape the presidency to the point where an individual president has little chance to develop his own style?

"No. It's true that there are patterns and traditions. But Princeton doesn't run on the basis of detailed directives from the president or anyone else. It is less hierarchical than most similar institutions. A large number of people are responsible for making decisions here. In one sense, we are all kibitzers here, encouraged to take an interest not only in our own special area but in all areas. This permits a genuinely collegial mode of operation. For example, both the dean of the chapel and the general counsel sit on the president's cabinet that meets weekly.

"We derive a sense of unity, I think, a sense of being knit together, from the university's basic character. This is reflected in the way we are able to adapt, and evolve, while holding onto first principles. When we became coeducational, we resisted the idea of a coordinate college, or of a separate dean of women, but insisted that women be included in the life of the university on the same terms as men, so the unity of the institution would be preserved. And I think that our judgment on that question has proved correct."

What about Woodrow Wilson? Is Bowen conscious of his influence on the presidency?

"Oh, I think all of us at Princeton feel an institutional kinship with him. We are his descendants, the beneficiaries of his ideas. But we are descended from James McCosh, too, who made this a university."

Bowen does not, we gathered, in confronting every crisis ask himself "What would Woodrow Wilson do?"

He laughed. "Emphatically not. The influence of a man like that is powerful, but subtle. We each have to do things in our own way in our own time, with a clear sense of current objectives.

"There is a basic sense of mission here so pervasive and powerful that we don't have to begin each day proclaiming it. The influence of Wilson is so evident that we don't have to overdo the explicit announcement of it, and that is, in a way, the greatest compliment we could pay him."

One more question, and he could get back to reviewing the Economics 101 midterm exam papers spread out on the conference table of his Nassau Hall office: With all its emphasis on instruction, has Princeton come up with some original principles of teaching that might be generally applied?

"Well, one, it's very hard."

Why?

"Because it depends not only on a continuing mastery of one's subject but also on thinking about how one communicates, and developing one's own style; on being willing to take the time to *listen,* and engage another person, the student, in serious intellectual discussion. Students don't come here expecting simply to write down what the teacher tells them. They come expecting to argue—to participate in the learning process, not just to be recipients. They see education as a two-way process. In my economics class, I work very hard to get students to explain the principles to themselves and to each other. The test of whether one has learned something is whether one can explain it.

"Learning and teaching involve respect for thinking; acceptance of the work it involves; a determination to pursue questions. Obviously, to be a learner or a teacher, you have to enjoy such interactions. Friendships often grow out of shared intellectual interests. Learning has its solitary moments, but it is not a solitary activity."

"The quest for truth—or rather for alternative versions of the truth—should be nonrancorous. It's conducive to good teaching and learning if people who disagree do so agreeably."

3

MARVIN BRESSLER

arvin Bressler said he would talk only about the Princeton differences deriving from its relatively small size and special atmosphere. Atmosphere being the harder to describe, would he start with that? How had Princeton struck him when he first joined its faculty?

"Coming here from NYU, with its center in Greenwich Village, where I was sensitive every day to the subterranean violence of the city, I was impressed by several differences. First, by what I can only describe as Princeton's serene sense of self-sufficiency; as if the university were an independent duchy—complete with its own foreign policy—which carried on diplomatic relations with other sovereign powers such as the United States of America."

He was impressed also to encounter here "the joys of competence. Princeton seemed to do things so well. I had the feeling that if the president—then Robert F. Goheen—were to form an ad hoc committee selected at

---

A graduate of Temple University, Bressler earned his Ph.D. at the University of Pennsylvania, where he taught sociology, as he did at New York University. At NYU he was chairman of the Department of Educational Sociology. He has been a professor of sociology at Princeton since 1963, and twice chairman of that department. He was also chairman of the Commission on the Future of the College, which spent two years examining undergraduate education at Princeton and comparable institutions.

12

random to plan, say, an annual picnic, no one on it would say anything stupid.

"At the same time, Princeton appropriately enough seemed to have some of the characteristics F. Scott Fitzgerald had as a novelist. I regard Fitzgerald as a better artist than is generally acknowledged. He wrote dialogue on the ordinary details of human housekeeping that somehow, on another level, expressed hidden truths about his characters.

"In much the same fashion, when I attended meetings, went to parties, or engaged in tennis post mortems with colleagues, the most casual observations seemed to me to carry significant implications; to be rooted in historical memory; to rest on a sense of a Princeton community which I didn't yet share. The others knew the code; I hadn't mastered the anthropology of the place, didn't know its heroes and taboos."

For example, during his first days at Princeton he attended an orientation session on the preceptorial system. It was conducted by James Billington '50, then a professor in the history department, now director of the Woodrow Wilson Center in Washington, D.C. "Jim spoke in fervent, Wagnerian tones. I struggled to understand the special mystique of preceptorials. They seemed to me indistinguishable from the small discussion sessions with which I was familiar at other institutions. Finally it dawned on me that what at first glance seemed merely a sensible pedagogical device was, in Jim's mind, an extension of Woodrow Wilson's biography—and that precepts, therefore, represented a kind of homage to American history. This recognition made an otherwise incomprehensible performance meaningful, even moving."

If he, Bressler, were describing preceptorials today to a group of incoming junior faculty, would he be Wagnerian?

"Absolutely!" He laughed. "I think it's characteristic of Princeton that one begins to share its ethos very quickly—or never. 'Ivy may be the fastest growing plant known to man,' and the soil in New Jersey is particularly fertile."

Is this important educationally?

"Yes, I think so. But my views stand at the intersection of love and irony. On one hand, I think our intense self-consciousness, our invincible conviction that we are a chosen instrument of a higher purpose, and our insularity, are an invitation to satire. But it is partly because of these excesses that we are able to realize our most ambitious conceits. Nothing truly great was ever produced by people with a flawless sense of proportion. The writers we honor in the history of social thought— for example, Smith, Marx, Pareto, Freud, Veblen—all 'went too far,' took their ideas to their outer limits. The best institutions are like that.

"If Princeton had had a more accurate sense of its location in the cosmos, its very real achievements would have been far less substantial. During the discussions on coeducation a decade ago we sometimes behaved as if we were about to bring forth a startlingly radical educational innovation—although most American colleges had been coeducational for more than a half-century. It was not just 'Should we admit women?' but 'Should WE admit women?' While it's easy to lampoon our exaggerated sense of self, I secretly hope the Princeton mystique will survive."

He was silent for a moment. Then: "I've often wondered why Norman Thomas, John Foster Dulles, and Adlai Stevenson came back for reunions year after year and put on funny hats. I'm not sure. But I do know that such strikingly different people—in both political conviction and temperament—shared a dedication and loyalty to Princeton, and a desire to convey to succeeding generations that the experience here was infinitely precious. Not long before his death, Thomas cut short an interview about the Vietnam War on the stated ground that it was time to listen to the Princeton-Dartmouth football game. Norman Thomas! The process by which such things happen is mysterious. The Alumni Council capitalizes on it but didn't invent it."

What is the source of this mystique?

"Well, it is in part aesthetic: the beauty and agelessness of this campus, whose physical setting has a kind of inevitability and whose buildings seem to have been here eternally, evoke in most of us a sense of continuity with the past. We've all had sentimental memories of places where important things happened to us, only to discover, on returning some years later, that the actual site has all but disappeared. Not so at Princeton, which is wholly recognizable as the place it was when first encountered."

Has Princeton's attitude toward itself, and the feelings of affection and loyalty this seems to engender, a bearing on the university's ability to educate young men and women and discover new knowledge?

"Yes."

How?

"This university is *serious*."

Meaning?

"Meaning endowed with the dignity that comes from confidence in its mission—the conviction that a university is the keeper of the books, responsible for preserving, extending, and transmitting their treasures."

Isn't this true of other institutions?

"Sure—but not to the same degree, because most don't have the same certainty of the validity of their announced purposes."

As to differences resulting from Princeton's size, Bressler cited seven.

"First, Princeton is probably the only university, in or out of its own class, in which the fundamental unit of loyalty, for the faculty, is the university itself and not one of its departments. Clark Kerr once defined a university as a group of private entrepreneurs loosely held together by common parking grievances. This emphatically does not describe Princeton.

"One tangible consequence of this unity is seen in faculty appointments. When a department is considering adding a new person, it takes into account the consequences this would have for the whole university. It makes a serious effort to get someone who will enrich not only its own work but that of other departments. This is one reason Princeton's interdisciplinary efforts are much more extensive than one would guess from merely observing its structural arrangements, and stronger than those at most other institutions.

"A second significant difference related to size is the absence here of the automatic antagonism between faculty and administration which exists at larger universities. Where you know one another, where people have faces and not just titles, where the president calls faculty members by their first names in general faculty meetings, it is difficult to project a world of heroes and villains. And of course the low level of hostility results also from the way size affects decision making."

How is that?

"More democracy is possible in a place where people know each other, where they relate as human beings and not as desks or offices talking with each other or, more likely, writing memos." He spoke of one huge corporation "in which you can tell by the water pitcher in an executive's office—gold-plated, silver, pewter—where he or she stands in the power structure. Princeton is at the opposite extreme. Here the fact that so-and-so is a dean and so-and-so an assistant professor tells you very little about the nature of their relationship.

"All of this is strengthened at Princeton by the processes of participation and consultation. There is full discussion of even fairly minor matters, involving a special vocabulary developed for the purpose. When it seems politic to discuss something with a superior, you 'run it by' him or her; when dealing with someone at your own level, you 'touch base'; and if you have to consult somebody really ominous, say the students, that's called 'testing the waters.' In the course of a day here there is a fearful amount of by-running, base-touching, and water-testing—some of it purely pro forma—but the result is that final decisions are not *imposed* on you; you have a chance to influence policy.

"There is an extraordinary degree of civility here among people who disagree strongly on issues. People arranged at different points along the spectrum, politically or ideologically, rarely transfer their feelings into personal enmity."

In contrast to other universities?

"Yes. I've discussed this with colleagues on many campuses and the situation just doesn't prevail elsewhere."

And is this significant educationally?

An emphatic nod. "It's the way scholarly disputation ought to be conducted. The quest for truth—or rather for alternative versions of the truth—should be nonrancorous. It's conducive to good teaching and learning if people who disagree do so agreeably." He said Princeton's atmosphere of civility is the more remarkable "when one considers that a university is a very difficult institution to administer because of the large number of constituencies all with equal—and insistent—claims on limited resources. What goes to one frequently has to be taken away from another, so everybody is more or less sullen all the time, at some subliminal level. At most institutions it isn't subliminal."

Bressler's third point was that because Princeton has emerged in recent years as a great research university—"in the fullest sense of having become a national intellectual force"—without greatly increasing its size, "it has resolved a common dilemma for both faculty and students: Do I want a small liberal arts college with its emphasis on teaching, or a major university with its commitment to research? Princeton is unique in offering the virtues of both with the drawbacks of neither."

The fourth difference: "Faculty members here tend to know more students than at larger places; know them as an extension of the family norm. And because your relationships are familiar and not impersonal or institutional, you tend to care more about the outcome of policies, to give more careful thought to your own role in formulating them. As institutions become larger, and their boundaries can no longer be seen, one's sense of personal responsibility and obligation tends to decline."

Point five: "A university of Princeton's size, because a lot of people do understand it in its totality, is *manageable*. A discussion involving six or eight people can begin a movement that ends in actually solving a problem."

Point six: "The mode of social control. Faculty and student behavior is governed not so much by specific regulations as by responsiveness to community opinion. People heed campus norms because everybody is so *visible!*"

Point seven: "Princeton's size has helped it in recent years to respond effectively to the changed composition of the student body. The welcome addition of women and racial, ethnic, and religious minorities to what had previously been a virtually exclusive preserve of wealthy WASP families has made the life of the campus more broadly representative of the wider society and has enabled members of diverse groups to gain a more complex appreciation of both the resemblances and differences among humankind."

But hasn't that happened at most institutions in Princeton's class?

"Let me put it this way: At Princeton, some students are offended by particular corporate practices adopted by the university, others feel alienated from campus life, and some groups believe that they suffer from academic neglect. These are terribly delicate and difficult issues, but they are mostly approached here in a spirit of trust and forbearance fostered by the small size of this community.

"As a result, Princeton has been able to respond to the needs of various constituencies tolerably well, given the constraints imposed by its financial and intellectual resources, and in a manner consistent with its traditions. By contrast, some other institutions either have been insensitive to altered conditions or else have changed dramatically—and not always for the better."

Bressler had to leave for a class, and on our way out I noticed on the back of his hall door a large poster of a Chinese basketball player. He explained it was a gift from President Bowen, brought back from his 1974 visit to China. "First time I felt a sense of solidarity with a 'Red Guard.'"

Reminded that Bressler is a sports fan and a close friend of basketball coach Pete Carril, I asked if he perceives anything singular about Princeton's approach to sports.

"Not only is there a higher level of participation in sports here than at most places but, more significantly, athletes are fully integrated into the student body—they are not a separate cadre who have 'come to play ball.' But talk to Coach Carril. More than anyone else I know, he personifies the simultaneous respect for learning and athletic achievement. I've long thought that despite obvious differences in background and vocation, Pete Carril and Robert Goheen actually have much in common."

To wit?

"A kind of monumental integrity, enormous competence, an overwhelming commitment to the work ethic, and the conviction that character is to be cherished over talent."

I phoned Carril and set up a date.

"A good teacher, whether in a school or a machine shop, has regard for the mind and soul of the student...: 'You respect me, I respect you.' American leadership must have this."

4

J. DOUGLAS BROWN

"Liberal education is not content, but process," said J. Douglas Brown. "A great mistake made at some of our sister institutions has been to think liberal education means taking certain courses. I've visited them. A professor up on the rostrum unloads on his students, and what he says may be profound and valuable, but liberal education is *the way you deal with students.*

"A person doesn't learn tennis by standing up and having balls knocked at him. There is no impression without expression. The classics are generally thought of as important elements in a liberal education—but they may not be liberal at all unless they are taught in a liberal way.

"It has been a Princeton tradition not to depend on dogmatic statements by professors, but to encourage students to discuss, to come back with questions, to use

Though he earned his A.B. (1919) and Ph.D. at Princeton and spent most of his working life there as economics professor, dean of the faculty (for twenty-one years), and provost, Brown has been a lifelong student of other universities and human organizations in general, as his best-known books attest: *The Liberal University: An Institutional Analysis* and *The Human Nature of Organizations.* He was one of three major architects of the Social Security system under Franklin Roosevelt, a trustee of the University of Rochester and Princeton Theological Seminary, and a director of McGraw-Hill. He was eighty and had been retired for two years when this conversation took place.

a variety of books. The professor doesn't assume he's the master and the authority, but his function is to open doors to students, so they can make up their own minds."

He said the Princeton undergraduate curriculum, "going all the way back," has been well organized. "And in modern times it was not Woodrow Wilson alone who put his mark on it, though he made a great contribution with his introduction of the precept system. When Luther Eisenhart was dean of the faculty (1925–33), he set up an undergraduate plan of study whose best feature was that it called for, in the first two years, breadth—to see the world as it is, see what science is, and history, literature, and so on—before narrowing into a special field. This makes for a better educated person for any career—business, law, even medicine—because it arouses curiosity in more than a single speciality. There is great danger to personal development in specializing at too early an age.

"A student once asked me to release him from all studies except chemistry; he intended to become a chemist and didn't want to waste time on other subjects. I insisted he take a course in history. He fell in love with it and became a history professor!

"Unity of the educational enterprise is an outstanding characteristic here. You find it also in the way underclass work merges into upperclass, and upperclass into graduate work, for those who go that route. An Oxford don once told me he'd rather get a student with a Princeton A.B. than one from any other American undergraduate college because he has already developed his own interests; his intellect and curiosity are already aroused by teaching that has not been dogmatic.

"Princeton's emphasis on the individual goes back a long way, to the college's very beginnings in the 1700s." He took from his bookshelves a slim volume—*The Princeton University Library in the Eighteenth Century* by the late William Dix, longtime librarian of the university—and read aloud from a 1752 document by Aaron Burr, Sr., the college's second president:

> It may be said, without any intention of disparagement to other learned seminaries, that the governors of this college have endeavored to improve upon the commonly received plans of education. They proceed not so much in the method of a dogmatic institution, by prolix discourses on the different branches of the sciences, by burdening the memory and infusing heavy and disagreeable tasks; as in the Socratic way of free dialogue between teacher and pupil, or between the students themselves, under the inspection of their tutors. In this manner, the attention is engaged, the mind entertained, and the scholar animated in the pursuit of knowledge.

"We've always stressed the growth of the individual, the enhancement of his powers of analysis, evaluation, organization. Now how do you treat individuals as individuals? By making them responsible. For example, the junior paper is an important piece of independent work, preparing the student for the senior thesis. Many students say they learned more from their senior theses than from any other aspect of their Princeton education. Why? It's not primarily the subject matter. It's the experience of getting hold of oneself and doing an arduous job that involves analysis, evaluation, decision making, all leading to the development of judgment. This is the sort of thing that matures a person.

"There is—always has been—a lot of interplay here between faculty and students on an individual basis, made possible by the high ratio of faculty to students, higher than at any comparable institution. The fact that seniors have carrels in the library is both symbol and evidence of Princeton's concern for individuality.

"I remember one spring while I was an undergraduate, an English teacher said to me, 'Brown, your ideas are all right, but you need to learn how to write. If you will do some writing over the summer, I'll read it, and work with you on it.' He did—and it probably changed my life. That sort of thing still goes on at Princeton.

"From a human-organizational point of view, interest in—and emphasis on—the individual, in all kinds of relationships, results in affection for and loyalty to an institution: a special attitude of mind and spirit. It isn't thought of as just a place from which you take what you think you need and get out, without ever looking back. If you've been treated as an individual, you will respond with loyalty, whether to a regiment, a football team, a corporation, or a university.

"I don't like to call Princeton unique in this—just say it differs from most of its sister institutions in putting more emphasis on it; and on dealing with its faculty as individuals, too. And the result is a high degree of loyalty among them as well.

"And because it's a 'single' faculty there is no divisive barrier between teachers of undergraduates and of graduate students. Also, Princeton has a very liberal sabbatical policy: We don't wear 'em down just teaching; we find out early if somebody has the necessary interest in scholarship by encouraging leaves to do research and writing. Of course there's strong institutional self-interest in this: When a faculty member takes a leave and comes back with nothing, well, that suggests he's not a creative scholar. Those fellows wear out, like a carpet does; whereas the creative person is self-renewing, like a good lawn.

"Teaching at Princeton is more demanding than at most places. In 'precept' teaching you have to be much better prepared than if you're merely lecturing, because you're not in control of what will be discussed. It's more interesting and more satisfying, but can be very tiring, especially as the students get brighter and brighter."

He said both faculty and students "feel like individuals" at Princeton because it is small enough so that people are "within sight of each other."

But aren't there disadvantages in smallness—such as fewer courses to choose from? "This can be a disadvantage in some cases," he acknowledged, "but our students can in effect 'create' courses. A senior can choose a thesis topic and have as his or her adviser a faculty member who is highly qualified to teach that subject even though he or she is not formally teaching it at Princeton. This gives amazing flexibility to the curriculum."

He volunteered that avoiding smugness is a problem for a university with Princeton's virtues.

Does Princeton avoid it? He laughed. "Yes."

How?

"Luckily for us there are Harvard, and Yale, MIT, Stanford, Cal Tech, and other great universities out there: many good keys to many good locks. We're kept modest by knowing that because of their sheer size they can do things we can't; and by having to compete with them for faculty and students—and not always winning!"

*   *   *

Not long after that conversation, Dean Brown, at 80-plus, moved from Princeton to a "retirement community and health center" in nearby Hightstown, where I visited him at intervals to talk about Princeton and this book. On one occasion I said the more I learned about Princeton's inner machinery—its emphasis on respect for the individual, its dealing with people in small groups, its insistence on consultation-before-decision, for example—the more I wondered whether Princeton might be a model for American industry to study in its current struggle to improve productivity.

Better, maybe, than the Japanese models then getting so much attention.

He was lying on his side in an infirmary bed, but his visible eye lit up. "The fact is, Japanese and American people are so different we can't learn much from them about how to deal with our labor force. They have traditionally, going a long way back, preferred confinement to insecurity. Americans, with some exceptions, are not that way. Individual freedom is a deep-down craving here. We're a country of people who want to maintain individuality and mobility; probably the least conforming people on earth. I was visiting England once, and my friend wouldn't let me wear a cap. Said, 'You look like a Yorkshire coal miner!' Japanese workers carry over the same loyalty to their employer that they once had to the emperor. America's population is drawn from people who rebelled.

"Princeton's way of organizing itself and dealing with its 'work force'—of faculty and students—reflects this American difference. So, yes, I'd say American business could learn a lot from studying Princeton, including its attention to the *look* of the place it asks people to work in; and its recognition that faculty will take things from other faculty they won't take happily from administrators; and that a good teacher, whether in a school or a machine shop, has regard for the mind *and* soul of the student, has integrity in that relationship, a mutuality of interests: 'You respect me, I respect you.' American leadership must have this."

"The only way to get out of here without hard work is to cheat, and that's illegal." 5

PETER J. CARRIL

A university is known to some extent by the coaches it keeps, and Princeton had kept Pete Carril as its basketball coach for fifteen years. Believing this must imply significant compatibility between his coaching methods and the university's educational philosophy, and that a talk with him might reveal facets of Princeton's character not visible to more conventional observers, I dropped in at his Jadwin Gymnasium office and asked whether he coaches according to some set of basic principles for achieving the teamwork that distinguishes Carril teams.

"Yes," he said. "There *are* four or five things that dictate my philosophy of coaching." After a few thoughtful puffs on his ever-present cigar, he began to lay them out.

Number one: "The most important thing you can do is what you're doing when you're doing it. I ask players, 'What do you stand for when you cross the line onto the court?' When you're out there, basketball should be the most important thing. When you play, *play;* when you study, *study.* Then it's not hard to separate the two.

"A second principle is, I try to tell 'em we are all creatures of habit. Good habits are hard to break and so

---

A graduate of Lafayette, Carril coached basketball at Easton and Reading high schools, and taught government and economics at the latter. After one year of college coaching at Lehigh, he became Princeton's basketball coach in 1967. Despite admission standards that have caused the rejection of "guys who would have made me famous," Carril has produced teams whose teamwork has made him famous, in both college and professional coaching circles.

are bad ones. I try to get 'em to understand: If they learn to do things right, or well, that gets to be the way they do things, and whatever happens, that's not going to change.

"Somebody once asked Fred Astaire when he was practicing, 'Why do you work so hard?' He said, 'To make things easy.'

"Punctuality is a good habit—for its own sake, and because when you're on time, and especially when you're *not*, you're telling your teammates what you think of them.

"Third—this pertains to basketball, but also to other activities: Do something that helps someone else, and then when it comes to doing something for yourself, it's easier to do." He let me puzzle over that for a minute.

"It's a point I haven't had too much trouble putting across at Princeton, but I have had trouble with it at kids' basketball camps and coaches' clinics. The idea is, you're on offense and you have the ball in hand and only one idea in mind: to do a certain thing yourself. You alert the defense to what it is you're trying to do, and that makes it harder for you because they're going to try to stop you. But when you have the ball in hand and you're ready to do *other* things, like pass to another player, set a screen to help another player score, make a hard cut, then the defense has to try to stop all those possible things and not just you and your thing. It's amazing how this idea comes out in a game. One thing that worries me about basketball today is the disappearance of the cerebral or mental element, the obviousness of the attack: 'Here I come! Try and stop me!' Each guy intent on doing his own thing.

"Here at Princeton the players are smart. They understand you have to take advantage of your strong points, adapt to your environment. We don't have the big guys, the stars, so we have to make the best of what we have. Our game takes a tremendous amount of understanding of what you're doing. And something more. It gets down to, 'What and who do you love?'"

The real fun of being a coach, for Carril, "is to bring twelve guys closer together. The better you understand that, the better they play. It's hard to do this with people from divergent backgrounds, with different goals and ideas on how to accomplish something, and being pressured by parents, friends, girlfriends; hard to get them to behave for the common good. You do it by becoming closely attached to each one, which depends on their ability to let you do that, and your ability and willingness to do it. If you run into a player with a low degree of caring, you can't become attached. But with the guys who give something of themselves each day, that makes for a happy experience for everybody.

"It's hard to believe the great feeling our players have for one another, the fellowship and love and respect, the total harmony there is among them. As a result, the way they play is not only good-looking and stylish, but effective as hell." But, he said, it takes hard work. "You can't have it by doing sloppy work, with a low degree of trying and caring."

Carril respects Princeton because it works its students hard academically. He likes that not only because he reveres hard work but also because it means the basketball players who choose Princeton are not afraid of hard work.

In recruiting high school students, Carril stresses Princeton's academic challenge. "Some coaches use a list of how much their graduates are earning. I've never done that. And of course they have big athletic scholarships to offer. When I talk with parents about the financial sacrifices they'll be making if they send their son to Princeton, I say, 'You have to work so hard at Princeton, to learn to do so many things by yourself, when you get out you can *produce* because you can *work*.' Students know they'll learn and grow here. That's why they pick Princeton.

"I remember when Mickey Steuerer ['76] was here, we'd sit and talk about how tough Princeton is. Things become so rough, so unreasonable, so demanding, but what's amazing is, the end result is just the opposite of what you might think: instead of getting to hate the place, you end up loving it, and as the years go by, instead of diminishing, the love grows!" Pause. "The harder a thing is, the greater the feeling of reward for having done it.

"Everybody has to do a senior thesis here—even most engineering students, where the load is so heavy you'd think they'd end up killing themselves!" That evokes awe and admiration in Carril. "Everyone here is an honors student. I coached Gary Walters ['67] in high school, and one of my remembrances of my first year here was waiting for him to come out of Green Hall the day he got the grade on his senior thesis. The look of accomplishment on his face!—enough power to light up any city! Greater than after any basketball victory!

"One reason Princeton alumni are so loyal is that they could have been shortchanged here, but they weren't. Oh, you could run into softness with a single professor, maybe, but it's not part of the system. I tell my players, 'The only way to get out of this place without hard work is to cheat, and that's illegal.'"

But he worries about the decline of respect for work in the U.S. generally. "Work used to be an attitude, now it's an ability; something you used to grow up knowing how to do, now it has to be learned. Our sports always reflect our society, so this shows up in college sports." Even at Princeton? He shrugged, then nodded. "Some potentially good players come here with a very superficial knowledge of the game. They've got the cart before the horse. The simplest things they don't find interesting."

Is Carril successful at turning them around? "I don't know. I think so. They get so they realize the importance of the intensity level. I've seen the way they grow."

He said he must seem "like a relic from another era" to them. "I'm willing to make some adjustments, but not basic ones. I don't like half-efforts or slovenliness, it just kills me—bad passes indifferently thrown…" He shook his head. "The guy who really doesn't care and shows it, that's OK. But when he pretends he cares and doesn't, that's hard to deal with.

"Maybe I make more of basketball than I should. Maybe it *is* 'just a game,' or an activity that for historical reasons is part of the college program but doesn't really mean anything, as in the case of England and Spain, for instance, where intercollegiate sports really don't mean anything. Am I going beyond what I should do? Should I stop and try to get a hold of myself?" He looked genuinely puzzled.

Back to principles.

"Number four has to do with fame, or notoriety, recognition. Somewhere along the line, some players get the idea this is a tremendous thing. But it's so unnecessary! You ought to do things for the right reasons: the satisfaction of integrity in performance, the pleasure after a hard-fought game, especially when you're the victor, of taking a shower, standing next to your teammates, talking about the game and how much fun it was—and what hard work!

"Fame comes out second, by far. Over the long run you forget all the clippings, but not the meetings in the shower, the great feeling of camaraderie.

"I noticed a couple of years before I came here, when Princeton played in an NCAA tournament in North Carolina, Duke and Connecticut and other schools had big bands and cheerleaders. Princeton had five guys sitting way up in the stands, where I was, playing 'Going Back.' They weren't even in uniform, and they told me they had paid their own way there. But there they were, playin' their hearts out!" He savored the recollection. Then: "To be known for making a shot is not as important as *making* the shot.

"I've only had a few players here who wanted to be famous. This is a bad place for guys like that, because every day here, somebody on the faculty does something that deserves worldwide recognition. That's going on all around you at any Ivy League college. It helps keep you down to size.

"I've worked here under two presidents—Goheen and Bowen—and neither was as well known as his counterparts in a lot of places. The reason is that they don't *want* to be. There's a tradition of modesty here, of doing your best each day in substance and not in the papers.

"It's something that runs throughout this university. And it's going against a national tide. People are climbing skyscrapers, parachuting down on 'em, jumping off bridges, to get attention, publicity. Here, we just do what seems natural to the institution. Princeton is the sum of a countless number of things being done by people content to operate that way.

"I remind my players: 'You're a part of that; take satisfaction for the real reason you're doing things.'"

Carril stopped. Would there be a fifth principle?

"No," he said. "If you follow those four principles you'll win a lot." And is that important? He gave me an odd look. "How else can you be sure you're doing things right?" He said Vince Lombardi's famous remark, "Winning is the only thing," has been misinterpreted. "He wanted his players to have good work habits, give it their best shot, knowing if they did they *would* win. You win by accident once in a while, but usually because you do the right things. Winning builds character; losing reveals things."

As he walked me out into the corridor I asked why he had stayed at Princeton fifteen years despite impressive offers from other colleges and even a pro team.

"Whenever I get an offer, I ask myself one question: 'What and who can you love?'

"There's nothing to love in the pros, not for me. When you come down to it, you can certainly love

Princeton and the people here. It embodies a strong tradition for excellence, and maintains high standards, produces easy interaction between people, from professors to roofers. It makes you feel humble, and for me that's good.

"I've had big-figure offers. I couldn't believe anybody would give me that much. But what would I do with it? Take a longer vacation, drive a Mercedes instead of a Dodge Charger, eat at swanky places, have people wait on me, wear more expensive suits, read the *Wall Street Journal* every day to see how my stocks are doing? What does money mean if you don't love your work? A very important part of my life is teaching—and they respect that a lot here.

"At some big-time basketball universities the emphasis is all on recruiting. 'Let's get a coach who can bring in the talent.' For me the basic thing has to be teaching. A guy in the sociology department at NYU, when he retired, told a reporter the kind of teacher he'd been. When I read it, I said to [sociology] Professor Marvin Bressler, 'That's a perfect description of me. The only difference is, I swear.'

"The real question is, why does Princeton permit a person like me to coach here? They could be looking for some tall, handsome dude, with the right image. Instead I'm this small little guy smoking a cigar and losing his hair."

Well, I said, why *do* they keep you?

He thought. "Basically I think it's because some of my players seem to be better for the experience."

"I want to show students—and encourage them to discover—what a wide variety of human behavior there has been over time and across cultures, so that they will be both realistic...and hopeful."

6

NATALIE ZEMON DAVIS

Having bicycled across the Princeton campus on a frosty October morning, Natalie Davis said it was hard not to open our conversation with a comment on the obvious: "...the beauty of the setting; the trees, the space. I really savor it. It provides the serenity and refreshment of soul so important to learning and thinking.

"Of course if setting were all Princeton offered I wouldn't be here, because I like the intensity of a city. But one gets some of that here, from having an excellent faculty concentrated in a small space; not only Princeton's but the permanent and visiting faculty of the Institute for Advanced Study. And New York and Philadelphia *are* handy."

As person and scholar, Davis said, she is fascinated by contrasts, and Princeton provides marked ones: "between its small size and its great stature; its bucolic location and sophisticated architecture; its tranquil air and the feverish intellectual activity that goes on here;

Before joining Princeton's faculty in 1978, Davis—B.A. Smith, M.A. Radcliffe, Ph.D. University of Michigan—taught at Brown, University of Toronto, University of California at Berkeley, and *Ecole des Hautes Etudes en Sciences Sociales.* Her books include *Society and Cultures in Early Modern France* and *The Return of Martin Guerre,* basis for an acclaimed French film on which she worked as historical consultant. Her published essays, in English and French, her editorships and professional society memberships are numerous and varied.

33

between its conservative, rather 'closed' past and its liberal, 'open' present. In fact these contrasts may be what most clearly distinguishes Princeton from similar universities."

When she left the Berkeley faculty to join Princeton's in 1978—"admittedly, partly to be nearer my husband, a professor in Toronto"—she did so with some misgivings, which were borne out on her arrival: "After teaching at Toronto and Berkeley I found myself in a place that reminded me of my alma mater, Smith College! Small and beautiful! I thought, 'Have I regressed?' But then I remembered how important Smith had been to me as a student; how grateful I had been for teachers who took me seriously, and personally. 'Where would I be now if not for them?'

"So I began to see Princeton as having some of Smith's good qualities *plus* an extremely good graduate program that made it a leading world university." And although her Berkeley colleagues had warned her that Princeton students "ran to type," she recalled that Smith, with a similar reputation for homogeneity, was much more diverse than met the eye. So she kept an open mind and was soon astonished at the range of types in the Princeton student body.

"They may look more alike than Berkeley students, who go in for costumes and actually do represent a wider class range. But Berkeley draws undergraduates almost entirely from California, and that leads to a kind of provincialism: an attitude that Berkeley is the center of the world; that whether the action is on campus or in city council, 'this is where it's at!'

"Princeton has students from a wider range of places, and there is a pretty good mix of social classes, races, religions. Actually, I've had more black undergraduates in my classes here than at Berkeley; and they're interested in *European* history, not just American. And the range of political views among students here is amazing."

She laughed as she recalled saying to herself on leaving Berkeley, "I'm going to the most *goyish* campus in America! I've got to teach at least one course that will shake 'em up!" She decided to propose A History of the Jews. "But when I got here I discovered such a course was already planned in Near Eastern studies, that there were kosher dining facilities on campus, and many other evidences of Princeton's openness." (She did eventually co-teach her course—on Jewish family and social life in the sixteenth through eighteenth centuries.)

As for women students, she had, of course, taught them at Berkeley, "but the ones I encountered at Princeton were somehow different for being a new element in an old place; had a special air of independence. There was even a girl who showed up in my History of Women class two years ago wearing a big 'Reagan for President' button. She turned out to be a feminist, too! Again, it was the contrast between Princeton's present and past that fascinated me. It's a kind of contrast that prompts a tension people can learn from."

At Berkeley, she said, "it's easy to be a radical, or almost anything else; easy to find a group of your own kind and lose yourself in it. Here the struggle for identity is more challenging—as it was for me trying to be a young radical at Smith—and I think that's great. And what's true of students is true of faculty members, too. Beauty aside, Princeton has a quite human dimension. One can physically get around, and know a lot of people. We see each other over and over in different circumstances: at meetings, on campus, at the supermarket, jogging. It makes for multi-layered relationships with colleagues—and with students."

Students often come to her house at the edge of the campus, and she sometimes holds classes there. "It makes for a flexibility and informality I associate with family life. Ideas get passed along—again with both faculty and students. Questions get asked at supermarket checkout counters and in the library stacks. Education and just living are not rigidly compartmented, thanks to the space here and the way one moves through it.

"But, as I said, as person and historian I'm always looking for 'corrections,' contradictions; and there is another side of the smallness coin. Sometimes you want anonymity; *not* to be always on tap, visible, gossiping or being gossiped about over the back fence. It's easy in a small environment, if you're not very careful, to fall—or get pushed—into a single line. We don't have that here. But it's a danger. In a larger environment, pluralism comes easier. It's harder to disagree freely with somebody you expect to bump into at a bicycle rack!"

Davis, who enjoys teaching and gets high ratings from students, approves of such Princeton traditions as the senior thesis and the custom of having senior faculty teach at all levels. "It's wonderful for the students and great fun for us; and encourages us to keep up with the young."

Do professors work harder at Princeton than at other research universities? "My guess is they do." She said she was currently teaching an undergraduate course— The History of France, 1500–1685—in which she does both the lecturing, twice a week, and the precepting. "That is, the thirty-six-person class is divided into three preceptorials of twelve each, and I meet three times a week with each group to discuss the material in the lectures and assigned reading." She was also teaching a graduate course, doing senior thesis advising and much informal advising, serving on various committees, meanwhile doing research for a book on "gifts in sixteenth-century France" and arranging for American publication of a book already published in France based on the screenplay she helped write for the French film *The Return of Martin Guerre,* which would soon open in the U.S.—to excellent reviews. Her off-campus lecturing was booked through the next two years. She had more time for all this, she said, now that her three children were over twenty-five. She said her schedule was not unusual for a Princeton professor. Walking her out to her bike I asked whether a one-time Smith College idealist and admitted do-gooder finds that teaching European history satisfies her urge to save the world. As she unlocked her padlock she said, "I feel what I'm teaching is infused with the quest for truth: of how people have lived in the past, of how important human values have evolved. I want my students to feel—and I believe many do—a commitment to carry life on as best they can, hoping and trying to make it better. I'm not a utopian. I want to show students, and encourage them to discover, what a wide variety of human behavior there has been over time and across cultures so that they will be both *realistic*—about people and societies, which can lead to a certain amount of pessimism—and *hopeful,* for which there is also some foundation in the past; not in a magical, wishful way, but based on reasonable possibilities.

"There is sheer delight, to me, in talking about the past, in relating it, as a story. Whether beautiful or troubled it's always engrossing. I like it when my students see how you can seize on the past and find something wonderful to think about there; feel some connection; some hope based on other people's experience.

"I haven't the same kind of urge to change the world that I had in my undergraduate days. Instead it's a combination of wanting to carry on, pass along the torch of culture to young people who may be able to make things better; and of having faith in human nature, no matter what.

"And it's nice to work so closely with students who go on, so many of them, into important and interesting and influential jobs. I don't just mean in the government; you can serve humanity in all walks of life. I'm impressed with the students who aren't taken in by facile careerism, who don't just want to conform. If I can help them feel a commitment to realistic hope, and be more creative in their work, whatever it is, I'd be glad. If I thought I was just training students who'd do what's safe, I'd be sorry. But my students don't seem to be that way.

"Princeton is a place where you can encourage both the ideas of service and of self-realization. It's a place where I can *be:* as a woman, Jewish, not automatically going along with the powers that be; where I can learn from my colleagues and from my students. I wouldn't go to a university just because the world considers it Number One, but only if *I* think it has great possibilities and if I can be myself in creative tension with it. I want to be an outsider and an insider at the same time; a part of the family but not swallowed up by it; and with all that I want it to have intellectual excellence."

And Princeton fulfills those requirements? She nodded, smiled, shook hands, and rode off into the leaf-gold morning.

"There have been substantial changes over the years...at Princeton, but not...in what the faculty has expected undergraduates to get from their studies."

7

JOAN STERN GIRGUS

"The careful and thoughtful way Princeton deals with its undergraduate curriculum" is what has most impressed Joan Girgus since she became dean of the college, responsible for key aspects of undergraduate life including the program of study, academic standing, academic advising, admission, and financial aid.

"There have been substantial changes over the years in what undergraduates have studied at Princeton, but not in the basic goals of a Princeton education; in what the faculty has expected undergraduates to get from their studies. Alumni returning decades after graduation can sit down with today's undergraduates and find a lot in common to talk about: a similar educational experience—which may help to explain why so many do come back!"

What are those "basic goals" of a Princeton education?

"We expect undergraduates to learn to think analytically and coherently; to express themselves in an

Before becoming Princeton's dean of the college in 1977, Girgus—B.A. Sarah Lawrence, Ph.D. New School for Social Research—was dean of the Division of Social Science at City College of the City University of New York. As professor of psychology there and at Princeton she has specialized in perception and perceptual development and is the author of numerous journal articles and (with Stanley Coren) of *Seeing Is Deceiving: The Psychology of Visual Illusions*.

39

effective way, both orally and in writing; to read with a critical eye, looking for the concerns and meanings that underlie the text; to appreciate the elegance of a mathematical or scientific proof, or of a clear argument; to stand by conclusions that have been arrived at in a thoughtful way; to realize that a certain amount of ambiguity is inevitable in most things; and finally to understand that decisions must be made—or the paper never gets written!

"Princeton has debated, through the years, the role of foreign language study, laboratory courses, mathematics, and so on. But there have been only two major revisions of the basic undergraduate curriculum in sixty years. Even minor changes—in the title of a course, or its number in the catalog—are carefully weighed both by the department proposing the change and by a standing committee of the faculty—the Committee on the Course of Study. Any proposal for a larger change goes through an extremely elaborate and extensive approval process. It is understood that nothing my office does, or the faculty does, is more important than keeping a careful eye on the curriculum."

Does this distinguish Princeton from its peers?

"There is seldom the kind of involvement of the entire faculty in the entire curriculum that is routine at Princeton."

She called it also distinctive for Princeton to devote as much attention as it does to pedagogy, "to the ways in which the curriculum is brought to the student."

"There is regular discussion, here, of how best to teach this or that discipline; of the appropriate format for each course. For example, most courses in the humanities and social sciences use a format of two hours of lecture and one hour of precept a week; but some need three hours of lecture rather than two, while others need two hours of precept—and some advanced courses are taught entirely in a seminar format. It depends on how the faculty believes the students can best engage the material."

Does Princeton think more about pedagogy than comparable institutions do?

She hesitated. "Woodrow Wilson was enormously devoted to undergraduate teaching, and the thoughtfulness he encouraged continues here as at no other major university. The turn of the century, when Wilson was Princeton's president, was a time of important developments in American higher education—elsewhere mainly on the graduate level, but here on the undergraduate level as well: a shift from the recitation-and-examination, memorize-and-give-it-back approach to the idea that students themselves can contribute to the discovery process that is such an important part of education. I had heard about the preceptorial system before coming to Princeton but had not realized how effectively it brings out not only the material but the student."

She had heard, too, about the senior thesis, but had not understood its significance until she saw "a thousand undergraduates—virtually the entire senior class—going through the experience every year. And I didn't realize how ambitious most thesis projects are—much more so than simply long term papers. Of course not every thesis is good, so not every student has this experience, but a remarkable number do. They learn how it feels to work, sometimes painfully, through a difficult and complicated analysis essentially on their own.

"I talked with a high school junior last spring at a school I was visiting. She wanted to apply to Princeton but was worried she might not be able to write a senior thesis. I said, 'Thousands have!—and lived to talk about it.' I tried to explain why the senior thesis is so important a part of a Princeton education. Finally, her eyes lit up and she said, 'I see! When you do your thesis, you learn how to become an expert in something; how it *feels* to become an expert!'"

In addition to its special emphasis on undergraduate teaching, there were three other Princeton characteristics that she said continually impressed her.

"One, the students here are not only very bright academically, but very talented. All this talent leads inevitably to an extremely rich extracurricular life."

Richer than at comparable places?

"There are surely as many talented undergraduates at other leading universities—but because Princeton is so small, the effect is more concentrated here, more intense. This is an important part of the Princeton atmosphere—and creates some tension, too, as all that talent seeks outlets.

"Two, the extraordinary interest and support of the alumni, who serve on schools committees recruiting students, and on career committees, and really *work* in these and other ways to generate a dialogue with students. And because alumni are a part of everyday life here they provide a kind of continuity. For me, knowing and working with alumni from the earliest decade of this century into the eighties has actually changed my sense of time. I now think over a longer span—and even feel younger because I see myself in relation to people who have lived much longer and yet are part of my life.

"I think undergraduates, too, feel this continuity; see themselves as eventually joining in the reunions P-rade as the latest in a very long line. When I talk with students about their—not infrequent!—requests for changes in the way something is done here, I remind them that decisions made at Princeton are expected to last for a long time, and they seem to understand that.

"Three, the campus: I still have days when I turn a corner or step out of a building and a sense of beauty washes over me. I care about surroundings, and all this"
—an encompassing wave—"is a visible reminder of the

thoughtfulness and caring that have gone into the building and maintaining of Princeton. It symbolizes what has gone on in the university generally. I think students, without always knowing it, take it that way. We all do. One hears students elsewhere complain about 'large, impersonal universities.' I don't think they mean only that the faculty doesn't know them by name, or that it's hard to get answers from an administrator. I suspect the buildings and trees of a campus also give messages, suggesting the kind of place it is, whether it's a place that is, and has been, cherished. The messages are not explicit, but they're there."

"When a school puts stress on its students to become active learners...that equips them—and reinforces their desire—to be responsible for other aspects of their lives."

8

ROBERT F. GOHEEN

One fall day in 1956 a thirty-seven-year-old assistant professor of classics at Princeton was called before the university's board of trustees and asked, "What do you see as this university's most distinguishing characteristics?"

His reply, as he recalled it for me:

"One, this is a small liberal arts college and a great research university in one; and, two, all of the faculty are teachers and scholars, not just one or the other, and all teach at every level, so that not only graduate students but undergraduates, even as freshmen, are engaged by the active, searching minds of scholars who take teaching seriously and don't just spew out a lot of facts and theorems and 'incontrovertible truths.'"

That must have been the right answer, because they forthwith made Robert Goheen a full professor and Princeton's sixteenth president.

Would he give the same answer today? Yes—but he would emphasize also "Princeton's concept that educa-

Born in India of American medical missionary parents, Goheen—A.B. (1940) and Ph.D. Princeton—served as U.S. Ambassador to India, 1977–80. He was president of Princeton, 1957–72, and then head of the Council on Foundations. Now a senior fellow of the Woodrow Wilson School, he is also director of the Mellon Fellowships in the Humanities. He is author of *The Imagery of Sophocles' Antigone* and *The Human Nature of a University.*

tion is something not to be passively received. All along, through a heavy schedule of written work and independent work, students here are challenged to become inquirers, responsible for their own learning. This is not unique to Princeton, but is at the core here to an unusual degree.

"At the collegiate level, anywhere, a student begins a process of search: to acquire facts and various techniques of organizing them and acquiring more. These are 'the tools of the trade,' and indispensable; but they are not the *end* of education, which is the deepening of understanding, the development of the spirit of inquiry. This is especially important in times like these when facts are so quickly outmoded. It's the urge and the ability to get at the facts, and the judgment to evaluate them, that we need.

"I can't prove this, but I believe that when a school puts stress on its students to become active learners, not mere recipients, to be responsible for their own intellectual development, that equips them—and reinforces their desire—to be responsible for other aspects of their lives. Again, Princeton is not unique in stressing this, but it *is* special in the way it supports it.

"What's difficult is maintaining a faculty of outstanding scholars who, as such, have an almost fanatical interest in their own subject matter and yet are deeply interested in students as learners; who get a bang out of seeing young minds grasp an idea or insight and carry it further than they, or you as teacher, thought they could. You have to know how not to overwhelm them with your own learning—while being there when they need you; know how to put questions in a form they can cope with, that doesn't stagger them, cause them to fall backward, lose their confidence."

Goheen would be going to Washington the following day to join in ceremonies welcoming Prime Minister Rajiv Gandhi of India. Had he during his ambassadorship to that country noted any parallel between teaching and diplomacy?

"Well, in both cases you're dealing with people of a 'culture' different from your own, you might say, and you must be able to get outside yourself and your 'culture' and be willing to listen, learn what's going on in the other person's mind and heart. So, yes, I guess there is a parallel, whether you're dealing with someone from another nation, another economic or social class, or a different level of academic achievement. In each case you need the ability to submerge, or at least temper, your own self-assurance and share the other's mind-set to some extent."

He stipulated, however, that "much can be learned, and I learned much at Princeton, from professors who were dominating and authoritarian, who simply knew so much, so well, that they were worth listening to. And we know that countries of the East, despite their rote methods of instruction, do develop formidable scholars and scientists."

Having served Princeton as professor, president, and now occasional teacher, how would he sum up its educational philosophy?

He said he would draw on his recollection of Alfred North Whitehead's *The Aim of Education,* and continued: "In the early grades, starting in prekindergarten, teachers work with the imagination, the restless curiosity and creativity of children. Later there must come discipline—step-by-step mastering of established facts and theories and methods. As Whitehead puts it, 'In education as elsewhere a broad primrose path leads to a nasty place.'

"Much of American higher education tends to put a heavy emphasis on discipline, but Princeton—like good colleges—believes there should be a process of synthesis, where intuition and imagination are called into play alongside disciplined thought, where independent inquiry and reflection are encouraged to test received wisdom. We believe students will do better for themselves and for society if at every stage, from prekindergarten to postdoctoral study, their creative and critical abilities are encouraged and nourished; if instead of being spoon-fed they are required to think for themselves.

"It's Princeton's policy to treat every student that way, though obviously not all are equally creative and critical. Other universities have honors programs in which a few students are so treated; at Princeton every student is."

Is there a connection between Princeton's educational philosophy and its having chosen to remain small for a research institution; that is, not to have professional schools of law, medicine, business? Yes, he thought so. "It goes back to Woodrow Wilson. He believed intensely in liberal education and the sorts of scholarship and research that relate to it, and felt that was Princeton's primary mission, where its major resources should be concentrated. He didn't even advocate a law school, though he himself had gone to one, at the University of Virginia. Wilson really had an enormous impact on Princeton. He may not have 'made Princeton what it is today'—other people had key roles in that—but it wouldn't be what it is without him. The preceptorial system was not his only contribution: He initiated a major strengthening of the sciences here that made possible, many years later, its becoming a major research university."

He conceded Princeton suffers some from the absence of large professional schools. "But there are offsetting advantages, especially in an age of intense specialization. We have a campus not only lovely but *integrated* in a way that provides more interaction among faculty members than is possible in larger, more complex universities. I've been reading an impressive report by a commission on graduate education at the University of Chicago. It stresses the importance of reaching beyond disciplinary limits to deal with overarching concerns—and they're increasing every day—that involve many disciplines. The report, it seems to me, talks Princeton's language.

"It is traditional at Princeton to be selective and 'build on strength' wherever possible, in the belief that 'quality is what matters, not quantity.' OK, we're an arts and sciences place, primarily, and when we reach beyond that core, then let's do things that relate to it. For example, the engineering school is highly scientific and theoretical as opposed to the day-to-day technical. The architecture school reaches out and draws on the capabilities of sociologists, political scientists, economists. The Wilson school, though it has a deliberate applied-public-policy bent, draws enormous strength from its shared faculty in the social sciences and other departments. These are Princeton's only professional schools—but they are not 'professional' in the usual sense because all enroll more undergraduates than graduate students.

"Even before the budget-cutting days of the late 1960s we studiedly forwent certain options because we couldn't see how to achieve them without sacrificing too much. It was a matter of personal regret to me, while president, that I couldn't move Princeton into South Asia studies, because that part of the world means a great deal to me. We had strong programs in Near Eastern and East Asian studies; there was a huge hole where South Asia might have been. But I became convinced that it was more important to maintain and extend the strengths we had than to fill that hole—especially as well developed South Asia programs were available next door at Penn and Columbia."

As president, Goheen had a close look at the relationship between a private university and its alumni;

now, as an ex-president, he could speak candidly about the phenomenon. Are Princeton alumni, reputed to be unusually loyal and supportive, also unusually inclined to be conservative and to put pressure on the administration not to change the old place they loved so well?

"There is that pressure," he said. "But the overwhelming majority of Princeton alumni take great pride in the quality of the university and want it to remain first-rate; do significant things; be a positive influence in the present and future. That pride works to offset the inevitable nostalgia."

"When you get good people and turn them loose to do their own thing, you get a depth and breadth of accomplishment that no autocratic type of organization can provide."

9

ROBERT G. JAHN

P rinceton has a well-respected School of Engineering and Applied Science, generally referred to as a "professional school," and at first glance this would seem to make Princeton like other research universities with their complements of professional schools. "But in fact," said Robert Jahn, "the Princeton engineering school is so different from professional schools generally, and interacts with the university in so unusual a way, that its presence probably makes Princeton more distinctive.

"Engineering education in the United States, and the world, probably covers a broader spectrum of styles and purposes than any other discipline. At one extreme are institutes that are frankly career-oriented, for professional preparation, the development of skills. At the other extreme is Princeton, offering surely the most

---

An authority on plasma acceleration and author of the standard text, *Physics of Electric Propulsion*, Jahn—B.S.E. (1951), M.A., and Ph.D. Princeton—taught at Lehigh and the California Institute of Technology before returning to Princeton in 1962. During his service as dean of the School of Engineering and Applied Science, 1971–86, the school's research budget increased by a factor of two and a half, its undergraduate population nearly doubled, and women and minorities were enrolled in substantial numbers. He introduced interdisciplinary topical programs to address social and economic problems from an engineering perspective. Jahn has served on several NASA advisory committees, as chairman of the board of Associated Universities, as a member of the board of Hercules Incorporated, and as a consultant to several aerospace corporations.

50

liberal engineering education one can find, addressing itself to the development of creativity through breadth of instruction and broad opportunities for independent study.

"Actually, we are not a 'professional school' in the usual sense: We are not engaged exclusively or even primarily in the preprofessional technical training of graduate students, as other engineering schools are. We do have graduate students—about 250 this year of about 1,500 in the Graduate School overall. But our larger component by far is undergraduates, and this is one reason for our unique interaction with the university. The numbers of these undergraduates—about one fifth of the entire undergraduate population—suggest that the impact of the school on the university's character must be considerable.

"The significance of this becomes clearer when you consider how tightly we are integrated into the liberal arts college. I know of no other first-rate engineering school that is so deeply involved in the academic and nonacademic aspects of its entire institution. Academically, our students are exposed to a broad band of creative humanistic and social science studies as a part of their programs. There is no area of undergraduate study in the whole university in which you are not likely to find an engineering student, or several.

"And the impact of these students—on fellow students and on faculty—is increased by their being extremely bright and articulate. Our freshmen typically have about a 725 average on their S.A.T. math tests, and verbal scores as high as those of their A.B. counterparts. Incidentally, many candidates for the B.S.E. are advanced placement students who can start their engineering education at a gallop. By the time they're seniors, many are doing the equivalent of graduate work.

"At the same time, not only do our high-caliber students rub elbows with non-engineers in classes all

over the campus, but we have everything from economists to Shakespearean scholars coming into *our* classrooms. This close association has to have a significant
effect in a university whose middle name is 'dialogue':
where interaction is stimulated in so many ways. Our
students have a different way of thinking, of approach-
ing problems, which they can communicate to fellow
students.

"This is probably true especially in interdisciplinary
studies such as those on the environment, on energy, on
transportation. But even in other courses—in politics,
history, and so on—it stands to reason that engineers
bring distinctive points of view. This is not to belittle
what our students learn from others. More and more,
engineers need a good grounding in economics, politics, sociology, and the humanities, in order, as they
move out into careers, to increase their versatility and
to better their chances of getting their ideas accepted.

"And in fact, about half of our B.S.E. graduates don't
go into professional engineering careers, but into medicine, law, business, and other sectors." Does this bother
him, that so many opt out? "Not at all! We cherish it!
They aren't dropouts but people who wanted an engineering background for a broad range of purposes. One
of the basic tenets of this school is that an increasingly
technological society demands people in every profession and occupation who have some engineering
literacy.

"In the past, high government officials, and decision
makers generally, didn't need much grasp of technological principles, but if they don't have it today,
they—and the country—are in trouble! We're pleased
that so many Princeton students understand this."

On the nonacademic side, he said, "you have engineering students rooming with biologists, Wilson school
majors, architects, you name it—and communicating in
ways not possible at schools where engineering educa-

tion is factored off to one side. They are very active in extracurricular activities, including sports. The number of our students in athletics is often disproportionately high, especially in baseball and football. And the concertmaster of the University Orchestra for 1979 to 1981 was an engineer. A woman engineer."

The faculty of the engineering school can be reasonably assumed to have a comparably strong effect on the university's character, he said, "not only because of their numbers [about ninety of a total of about seven hundred] but because of their high quality, and because in this relatively small place they interact more with other faculty members than their counterparts do at larger institutions. They play squash with professors of classics; at seminars they sit next to professors from a variety of disciplines. In interdisciplinary courses, and in university governance, there is an unusual closeness and interaction.

Would he call Princeton a "well-engineered" university?

"Well, I'd say it's run on sound engineering principles. It takes a complex problem involving entangled cross-disciplines—with sociological, economic, political ramifications—and breaks it down into component parts, assembles the resources to deal with it, and proceeds systematically to a solution. That approach is just as useful in running a university as in operating an airport. It has benefited Princeton immensely, and one likes to think engineers have contributed to that."

Given the Princeton engineering school's differentness, does it turn out a different kind of engineer?

"Yes, I think so. A disproportionate number of our graduates end up in policy-making positions. They're leadership material, and often this is quickly recognized. They are placed not in line assignments but in leadership, because of the breadth of their education, their having seen more of the humanities and social sciences than their counterparts at similar schools, having enjoyed rapport with students from all fields, and having been trained by a faculty that is more broadly based.

"I think they have a special respect for creativity. Those who become executives want to turn loose the imaginations of their better people, handle them more the way students are handled at Princeton; that is, schedule their work to give them more freedom to explore the byways and ramifications of their specialties; provide them with more dignity and independence; put less emphasis on rote. They understand, from their Princeton experience, that when you get good people and turn them loose to do their own thing, you get a depth and breadth of accomplishment that no autocratic type of organization can provide."

"Princeton, as a matter of institutional policy, in the way professors treat students, does the most to instill confidence in them."

10

SUZANNE KELLER

To Suzanne Keller, a sociologist with a special scholarly interest in male-female relationships, one thing that distinguishes Princeton is the way it teaches and encourages students to deal with complex problems, such as the "huge" one that most concerns her— "how to achieve a gender-equal society and congenial relations between men and women within such a society."

The first woman to receive tenure at Princeton, Keller considers herself extremely lucky to have been on the faculty when the first class of freshman women arrived in 1969, and to have witnessed at close range the shift from an all-male to a male-and-female student body.

"There is a saying in biology that 'ontogeny recapitulates phylogeny'—or, the development of the individual repeats the development of the species; the human being in going from embryo to birth recapitulates the evolution of the human race. As I watched women undergraduates arrive and make a place for themselves in a man's world, I had the feeling that here was the

Keller—A.B. Hunter College, Ph.D. Columbia—teaches undergraduate courses in design of communities, contemporary elites, the changing family, and sociology of the future, with emphasis on gender relations and the influence of space on human behavior. She also works with graduate students of architecture. She has taught at Brandeis, New York Medical College, Vassar, NYU, City College, and—as a Fulbright lecturer—at the Center of Ekistics in Athens, Greece. Her books include *Beyond the Ruling Class, The Urban Neighborhood,* and *Building for Women;* she is currently writing a book on "creating community."

women's movement in America taking place in miniature.

"The experience has given me a new appreciation of how difficult it's going to be for both men and women to reeducate not only their minds but their emotions to deal with equality."

She said the applicability of Princeton's educational philosophy to this broad societal problem struck her with particular force when she was preparing a magazine article for an editor who had asked her, on the basis of her scholarly work and many contacts with students, to suggest principles young men and women might profitably follow in relating to each other in this confusing, rule-less period.

"When I read over my suggestions I realized that the approach I was advocating to this one problem is the one Princeton advocates—not uniquely, but in an unusually concentrated way—to all complex problems."

What was that approach?

"I said to both young men and young women—who come to a relationship from different directions but with similar confusions— 'Acknowledge that you are dealing with a tough problem. Don't underestimate its complexity or its subtlety or the hard work you will have to do to solve it. Approach it with a flexible and open mind, confronting and admitting your own deep-seated prejudices—we all have them—that will have to be overcome. But finally, believe in your mind and heart that the problem can be solved and that you can solve it.'

"This element of self-confidence is enormously important, and of all the universities I know, Princeton, as a matter of institutional policy, in the way professors treat students, does the most to instill confidence in them; the feeling that they are not insignificant kids, undeserving of a full professor's time of day, but are in a sense the equals—or at least the respected junior partners—of the faculty, and as such have formidable problem-solving powers."

Was she suggesting that because of the way they're educated, male and female Princeton students have no trouble getting along with each other?

"Far from it! They may even have *more* trouble, because the more forthrightly one confronts this problem, the larger it gets. So much of it has been covered up for so long. I *am* saying that their liberal education gives them a handle on it and other personal problems if they will make the connection, which increasing numbers seem to be doing."

For her, light was shed on Princeton's character by the way it handled coeducation, "demonstrating that despite its traditionalism—its feeling that what it has done in the past is so excellent there can't be much need for change—once it decides to do something, it does it better than any other institution I know. Coeducation was a profound departure from more than two hundred years of tradition, but once it came, it came with speed and grace, thanks largely to the leadership of then President Goheen and then Provost Bowen, two men I greatly admire for their firm principles and ultimate flexibility."

She feels Princeton has been unusually successful in integrating women into classrooms and extracurricular activities, including sports, and that its educational arrangements—emphasis on liberal education, close faculty-student relationships, and so on—make it unusually attractive to women students.

Its record for hiring women faculty is less impressive, she said, but probably no worse than other universities of its type, and getting better. "Women are still by far the 'outgroup' as to numbers, but some distinguished and some promising women have been hired, and the outlook is probably good that more will be."

As for her experiences as Princeton's first tenured woman, she smilingly recalled that in the letter from the dean of the faculty advising her of her promotion she was inadvertently saluted as "Dear Mr. Keller."

She said, however, that she has encountered no rude behavior from fellow professors. "I was never accused of being stupid or incompetent, as the long history of an all-male faculty implied I might be; or at least not to my face. But individuals can escape that sort of thing, where a group cannot. When I first came, the men were very chivalrous: much holding-the-coat, opening-the-door sort of thing. And while it's not unpleasant to be treated that way..." She shrugged. But surely chivalry is better than hostility? She laughed. "It depends on what the chivalry masks—which may be hostility!"

But things are better now? "Oh, yes. One feels less conspicuous now. There is a freer exchange, more openness. As a result of coeducation, and the addition of even a small percentage of women to the faculty and a larger percentage to the administration and staff, the style of the university has changed. Not its basic character, but its demeanor; its atmosphere. Before, it was reserved: lots of closed facades; a definite dress and speech pattern. The ethos of the place was much more monolithic. To succeed here you had to adapt.

"Now there is a freer spirit, which I like better. It's more ecumenical. There is more wit, humor, less pretentiousness. It's more improvisational. I wouldn't have stayed at the old Princeton. Now there is more innovation, more insouciance."

More than at similar universities?

"Well, because of Princeton's size, any change is more pervasive and more recognizable here. So, yes, Princeton has probably changed more, and for the better."

"There is a tradition here of faculty members actually getting acquainted with students, talking things over with them."

11

STANLEY KELLEY, JR.

I n the turbulent late 1960s when American universities were being pressed by their students, sometimes violently, to share their decision-making authority, Stanley Kelley was chosen by the Princeton faculty to head a special faculty-student Committee on the Structure of the University.

For a full year, under his guidance, that group intensively studied how Princeton and similar institutions are run; who actually makes what decisions and how. It then made recommendations for extensive restructuring, most of which were adopted.

Princeton's approach to this problem was significantly different from that of similar universities, said Kelley, and revealed something about Princeton's character.

"Princeton anticipated trouble before it came, and took it very seriously when it did come. Some two years before student activists here began making demands for more say in governance, President Goheen, aware of troubles elsewhere, set up various committees to examine the role of students in decision making. As the pressure grew, he broadened the study. So students and everyone else knew the university was concerned."

More so than at other universities?

A professor of politics and former chairman of that department at Princeton, Kelley holds an A.B. and A.M. from the University of Kansas and a Ph.D. from Johns Hopkins, where he has taught. Before joining Princeton's faculty in 1957 he was on the Brookings Institution's staff. His field is American political parties.

"Elsewhere the self-examination tended to be more superficial, designed just to 'take some of the heat off.' Their committees were too large to function, their studies went on and on, the makeup of the committees kept changing so that very little was accomplished. Here, Goheen himself served on our committee, which was very unusual and indicated Princeton meant business."

Kelley's committee discovered "a lot of careful thought had gone into setting up Princeton's governance structure through the years."

Resulting in a structure peculiar to Princeton?

"Yes, in some important ways. First, and most striking, the Princeton faculty, long before the 'troubles' hit, was routinely taking an important part in running the institution. A professor at a university then in an uproar told me there had not been a meeting of the general faculty there since about 1810; that in fact there was no 'general faculty,' the faculties of the undergraduate and graduate colleges being separately organized.

"But Princeton, going back to before Woodrow Wilson, had been holding such meetings fairly regularly, and in recent years on a once-a-month basis. So we in effect already had a mechanism for dealing with such a crisis. We could immediately focus on specific issues while faculties elsewhere were wondering how to organize themselves to do so.

"And our faculty was—I hesitate to use the word— more democratic. Elsewhere, faculty committees were appointed by deans, whereas here they were, and are, elected by the faculty. There, general faculty meetings were restricted to tenured professors; here, junior faculty had long participated, on a one-person, one-vote basis.

"And the relationship between faculty and administration—the president and deans—was different here. I don't know about the eighteenth and nineteenth centuries, but Princeton in the twentieth never seems to have had a dictatorial president—such as Nicholas Murray Butler, whose high-handed ways caused friction between him and the Columbia faculty. The president here has long been seen as the leader of the faculty, as one of them, and most deans are seen as faculty members *serving as* deans. This is symbolized in faculty meetings where each dean has one vote as a faculty member. There has not been the 'us-versus-them' feeling, as in some California universities, for example, where the faculty meets separately and conveys its views to the deans and the president.

"The traditional role of students also was unusual here. The best example is the Discipline Committee on which students have served, along with faculty and administrators, and had a full vote, going back to about 1925. Some alumni and others thought it odd, our giving students that much voice in something so important. But the principle was adopted and digested long before the 1960s.

"There is a tradition here of faculty members actually getting acquainted with students, talking things over with them. So as the atmosphere heated up, groups of faculty members were already spending late hours talking with students—liberals with one group, conservatives with another—and this released a lot of pressure. In universities where faculty members commute to campus, and where the ratio of students to faculty is much higher, there is much less of that continuing, natural communication. There was also a lot of discussion among faculty members across the political spectrum here, more than in larger places.

"And confrontations were less bitter here because students had fewer grievances. I had an undergraduate research assistant about that time, a math major, very able student. He decided to do graduate work in statistics at a major California university, and before he had even completed a course in statistics they had him teaching undergraduates—statistics! The results were probably not bad, given his talent; but the thought seems outrageous to anyone here.

"The practice was not unusual at lots of places in the days of great increases in undergraduate attendance. The disparity between what a student expected, in the way of teaching, from a prestigious university, and what he actually got fueled a lot of resentment and hostility at other places; the feeling of having been 'conned.' The absence of that feeling here—and at Yale, which is close to Princeton in its attitude toward teaching—helped us when the 'revolution' hit.

"And students here didn't have the feeling that nothing could be done to improve their lot without radical changes in governance, because there had traditionally been more participation in student government here than at most places. Our students thought things could be changed by nonviolent means."

Anything singular about how his committee went about the restructuring process?

"Yes. At some universities a committee comparable to ours would ask, 'What is the proper role of the administration? Of the faculty? Of the students?' —as if decision-making power were a big pie to be carved up. Each group wanted the largest possible slice, and that maximized the conflict among them.

"Another approach, elsewhere, was: 'The students want more participation in university governance, so we will set up a committee to study their role.' Still another was, 'We need a university senate: who should be in it?'

"A fourth way—our way—was to ask, 'How is the university governed and how could it be governed better?' With this approach you ask, (a) 'How are decisions being made in various fields?' (b) 'Who might contribute to making better ones?' Obviously not everyone is interested in every type of decision, so you need very different mixes of faculty and students on different committees. The students sensibly saw some decisions as not of interest to them, others as beyond their qualifications to deal with.

"So you study the university, decision-area by decision-area, and then you ask question (c): 'What kind of institution can we design, or redesign, for the better making of all these decisions?'"

Out of that process was born the Council of the Princeton University Community (CPUC), with representatives from all university constituencies: faculty, undergraduate and graduate student bodies, administration, staff, and alumni, "a place where people can say what's on their minds, get informed of problems—including financial ones—at an early stage, and where those who make decisions are able to explain them to people who will explain them to others at their level.

"As a result of the governance restructuring, Princeton students are now involved to an unusual degree in many activities of the university once reserved to faculty. There are undergraduate departmental committees, and similar graduate student groups, that review departmental decisions and arrangements, and make their views known. At the university-wide level, students now participate in discussions held by the Faculty Committee on the Course of Study; they sit on the Priorities Committee, which makes recommendations on the university's budget, and on the Judicial Committee which hears appeals from, and deals with cases that exceed the jurisdiction of, any other disciplinary body."

With the "student revolution" over, does he feel the changes in governance remain useful?

"Yes. The increased student participation in nearly everything the university does is educational to those involved; and, through them, to students generally. This will surely mean an alumni body that understands how the university makes decisions. Given the extraordinary degree of alumni involvement in Princeton affairs, this is important.

"As Marvin Bressler has said, 'At many places the administration's assumption is that most faculty members are incompetent. Here the assumption is that they're all competent.' Underlying the restructuring here was the assumption that our students, too, are competent, and identify with the place and care about it, about upholding its quality."

"A little bit of isolation, such as Princeton's location gives it, does seem conducive to intellectual creativity."

12

ALVIN B. KERNAN

Most of Alvin Kernan's remarks had to do with Princeton in comparison with Yale and Harvard, and were made with a twinkle in the eye, a warning that he would overstate now and then, and the observation that "there are many different ways of baking a cake. The only question is whether your way works or doesn't—and they all do."

He began with location. "Princeton is in a small town that's *not* a small town, that appears to be easy-going, 'just folks,' turn-of-the-century—but behind the doors is something very different. That surface casualness, folksiness, hometowniness carries over to the university. Any dean, or alumnus, of the Graduate School can tell you how well hidden the professionalism of the place is. When I was dean I once overheard an undergraduate Orange Key guide lecturing a group of sightseers under my window in Nassau Hall—with not a word about the Graduate School!

"There is a pretense of amateurism that everybody here has to play out—back of which is the reality of the Graduate School and the research that is the educational

Kernan earned a B.A. at Williams, a B.A. at Oxford, and a Ph.D. at Yale, where he taught English for nineteen years, and was associate provost, acting provost, and director of the Division of Humanities before coming to Princeton in 1973 as dean of the Graduate School, a position he held for four years, and as professor of English. His books include *The Cankered Muse* and *The Plot of Satire*. He has been chairman of the Visiting Committee to the Harvard English department since 1978.

life of the place. But even those most deeply involved in it don't seem to want to *appear* professional.

"This is a point of real difference, particularly with Harvard, where the great professors are conspicuously involved in scholarship and research, and that's the role you're expected to play if you want to amount to anything. Harvard prides itself on its renowned scholars, distinguished people who give the place its international reputation. At Yale, the impression to be given is that you're unbearably busy. At Princeton, the appearance has to be the opposite: you have an infinite amount of time, are never harassed, even though the opposite may be true. You have to seem 'laid back.' It's not the reality but the role.

"If you want to occupy a visible, public position as The Great Scholar, Harvard is probably the place to go—though Yale and Princeton have many scientists and scholars as distinguished as anyone at Harvard; but to varying degrees at the former places the individual gets absorbed into the group.

"The Harvard system concentrates on hiring professors in their forties, after they've achieved reputations as scholars—elsewhere. It's a star system and it draws stars who've achieved stardom not primarily by teaching."

Turning to religious roots, he said the "established" religion at Harvard has been Unitarianism, at Yale Congregationalism, and at Princeton Presbyterianism. "The characteristics of the religions have transferred over to the universities and are still exerting an influence on them. Congregationalists were the sternest: everything bare and plain, dealing with fundamental realities. That high seriousness characterizes Yale's intellectual approach as well. Unitarians have broad interests, the wide scholarly outlook that Harvard cultivates—minimal doctrine and the avoidance of all bias. Presbyterianism, which originated in Scotland and very quickly became the state religion there, has closer ties to society. Not 'high society,' but the social order, to whose realities the Presbyterians have traditionally adjusted better than the Congregationalists or the Unitarians. This social orientation echoes in Wilson's 'Princeton in the nation's service'—or 'for' the nation's service; he said it both ways. Of course Yale's motto is the more metaphysical 'For God, for Country, and for Yale.'

"As for the personalities of the three institutions: A Harvard professor once said to me, 'We're like an old New England house—everybody has his bedroom and pretty much stays in it. Meals are brought on a tray. It's a house of seven gables; like Emily Dickinson's.' At Princeton some of the same things happen: Scholars tend to work at home a great deal. But the public scene is of a small town in which they're visible, which implies accessible."

Well, aren't they? To students, at least?

"Oh, sure. If you play a role long enough it affects you more than you affect it.

"One thing that's always intrigued me: The area in which Princeton distinguishes itself is primarily *theory*, not history or practice. This is true in mathematics, physics, philosophy—even music, which focuses more on the theoretical, or composer's, level here than on its history.

"This might seem at first to conflict with what I said earlier about Princeton's involvement with society; that is, we might expect that this involvement would lead Princeton to emphasize practical rather than theoretical matters, the actual history of men and things rather than abstract philosophical schemes. But Princeton is far more 'social' than Harvard or Yale—and now I *am* speaking in the 'high society' sense: more interested in the way people dress, the wines they serve, the quality of food, houses, international travel, manners. Princetonians are what you might call a very upper-middle-class intellectual set trying for an aristocratic way of life, or aristocratically-upward mobility.

"One characteristic of such a group is that it likes to deal with things in theoretical terms rather than do the day-to-day work of investigation or application at the level of working details. So it's in theory that Princeton is intellectually most active and effective. Physics and mathematics, not history and sociology, are our most distinguished departments. You realize, of course, that I'm overstating and oversimplifying?"

Yes. But was he suggesting it's desirable or undesirable to be the way he described Princeton as being?

He laughed. "I won't try to answer that. The argument has been going on since Plato and Aristotle. Sometimes it has been the historian whose work was considered most important, sometimes the theoretician. For some reason, though, a little bit of isolation, such as Princeton's location gives it, does seem conducive to intellectual creativity."

This emphasis on theory over practice is reflected in "the small number of professional schools at Princeton. And those professional schools it has—dealing with public affairs, engineering, and architecture—are more theoretical than most of their counterparts. When I came here from Yale I thought Princeton might be wise to add schools of law and of business; but I changed my mind. They wouldn't fit the academic ethos."

Does Princeton attract a type of student who recognizes and wants to sustain the characteristics he had spoken of?

"I believe Princeton is perceived as being more fashionable, socially, than the others. This is not true across the board, but by and large students here do dress more conservatively and are more polite. There is a softness of tone as compared to the hard-edgedness—and -edginess—at both Harvard and Yale, where students reveal a more aggressive quality in the classroom. Princeton is more civil."

As for undergraduate teaching at the three universities, "I wouldn't say it's better here, but it's distinctly different, and of high quality. The choice, for students, would depend on their own characters. If self-sufficient and highly individualistic and intellectually aggressive, Harvard or Yale; if they tend to function better in an academic *community* setting, then they're probably better off here. Someone is always watching here, seeing they don't get in too deep trouble. Harvard undergraduates educate each other in the light cast by mighty intellects. At Princeton they actually come up against senior faculty members. Teaching styles vary at the three places. But as to which is better"—he shrugged. "You can learn from both kinds. I recall learning a great deal from marvelous teachers who wouldn't give you the time of day."

With respect to administrative style, he found Princeton "clearly more efficient than either Harvard or Yale, mainly because of its smallness." He also found that Princeton has a "social" way even of resolving differences. "Confrontation is dangerous to societies and is avoided here. Things are more abrasive elsewhere. This place is kept together by reasonable compromises. I was surprised, when I came here, at the amount of careful private consultation that goes on before anything is openly discussed, much less debated and settled. But that fits the Presbyterian pattern. Being small, Princeton is more human, in that you can see people very readily, get answers more quickly. Yale and Harvard are no less humanitarian, but there the machinery grinds a bit more loudly."

"Learning can be painful...to be handed a hammer, then, as soon as you learn that, to have it snatched away and be handed a screwdriver."

13

AARON LEMONICK

D oes it make for a different kind of university community when you have a faculty as involved as Princeton's is in teaching undergraduates?

Aaron Lemonick thought, and nodded. "You probably end up with a body of people who feel a special sense of common mission. Whether you love it or fear it, teaching is personal, and exhilarating. It's a shared experience different from that of scholarship and scientific research."

How?

"As a scientist I don't really understand the research a scholar in the humanities does, because I haven't done it. But teaching is the same in every field; it's something we all do at Princeton, and take very seriously. We are a closer community because of that shared activity. I feel it when I meet someone who's never taught. I don't mean it makes us better human beings!" He laughed. "A community of shoplifters, or forgers, might be just as congenial!"

Lemonick was said to have strong views about the craft of teaching. What were some of them?

On completing high school in Philadelphia, Lemonick spent six World War II years in the U.S. Army Air Force, then earned his A.B. at the University of Pennsylvania, and his Ph.D. at Princeton, in physics, which he taught at Haverford College for seven years before joining the Princeton faculty in 1961. He has been chairman of the physics department and dean of the Graduate School, and was dean of the faculty at the time of our talk.

"To me there is a joy that runs through teaching, at three levels: The celebration, one, of what man has achieved in the past; two, of what the student before you has just achieved; and three, of what you have achieved by getting the student to achieve.

"But if teaching can be a joy, learning can be painful. Glorious, rewarding, exciting, yes! But not easy. Over and over to be put in the position of a fledgling; to be handed a hammer, then, as soon as you learn to use that, to have it snatched away and be handed a screwdriver."

He shook his head and shifted metaphors.

"I think of students as standing on the shore of a swamp they know they ought to cross, with the teacher as a guide. It's not enough for the teacher to say, 'Come on! Follow me!' It takes a certain amount of gathering them up spiritually beforehand. You have to explain: 'I'm going to be out of sight some of the time, but I'll be there, and you can follow me. You may be up to your armpits in sewer water, but you won't be in quicksand! And you won't be alone.'

"When I teach [as dean of the faculty he still teaches physics to undergraduates] I *become my students*. When what I am saying doesn't excite me I know it won't excite them. When I write out a lecture, I am telling myself the story as I write it. I put myself at the level of my students.

"In telling students about a discovery, you can't tell them every single thing that went into it. You have to make certain leaps, and whether you make them successfully depends on how well you understand your students."

He is known as a spontaneous kind of lecturer: but he does write out his lectures in advance?

"Sure—and then never refer to the manuscript. It's a way of organizing what I want to say." He adjusts what he's saying to how his students are taking it. For this, he has to keep his eye on them and be flexible and sensitive.

"I can tell I'm not doing well with a class when I find myself talking to the blackboard, or raising my voice, as people do when they talk to foreigners. In basketball, according to Bill Bradley, you need 'a sense of where you are.' Well, in teaching you need a sense of where *they* are."

He said he usually spends the first five or ten minutes of any class period "just getting them to come along— like a guide introducing people to some historic place. You try to give them a sense of the pleasure that's in store; the worship; the awe.

"The students who hate a subject, how do you get them to love it? Sometimes all you can do is make it plain that *somebody* loves it—*you* do—and they can love it vicariously through you. Sometimes the best you can do is say to a student, 'I'll give you a skill; make it possible for you to do a problem, or understand a thing that now seems hopelessly baffling. I promise you, if you come along with me, to give you something to take home.'

"You have to pace yourself by saving some of the surprises for later, some of the glory, to help motivate your students to be willing to go along with you through the dull and the trivial and the hard—like a novelist has to have suspense and surprises in his story to keep the reader interested through some unsurprising but essential parts.

"Sometimes I say to a class, 'I'm going to cover the whole blackboard just to show you that little "a" and big "B" are related. This will be a bore, but it's essential that you know this in order to get on to the interesting part.'"

What do you do when you feel you have lost the attention of a class?

"What you do when you lose your way anywhere! You ask questions: 'What's the matter, Harry? What have I left out?' If you have enough sense of your students, you know whose judgment to respect. If they tell you you're doing something wrong, you go back, and do a little soul searching."

Lemonick is not a permissive sort of teacher. "There has to be some giving on the part of the student. I have zero sympathy for the student who won't try to do the work. We've struck a bargain, he and I; we've made a pact. I will do my best for him, keep my side of the bargain. I will not make it harder than it deserves—than it needs—to be, as if there were some virtue in making it hard. But sometimes it has to be hard. It isn't all amusement. Then, if he won't keep his side of the bargain, if he won't *try*, I won't weep for him."

What are some characteristics of a poor teacher?

"A tendency to look down on students, show scorn for them, give them the impression they can't learn."

What about coldness?

"Coldness is all right. People who are cold by nature would be making a mistake to pretend to be otherwise. I remember being grateful that a certain teacher of mine didn't make jokes and try to approach us personally."

Why?

"I didn't like her! It would have been an unnecessary and distracting strain to have to be polite to her and laugh at her jokes. Still, I could accept her as a good teacher."

He especially disapproves of teachers who bully students by giving them more work than can possibly be done in the time allowed, and those who "pick on students, tear them down, rob them of their dignity, just to feed the teacher's ego. And it's almost as bad a mistake, if a less common one, to try to build up the egos of your students at your own expense. You've got to maintain your dignity as a person and doubly as a teacher, or you can't give them what you have to give them."

"Wilson said, 'There is a very real sense...in which the spirit of truth, of knowledge, of hope, of revelation, dwells in a place like this.'"

14

ARTHUR S. LINK

"**P**rinceton is the only university in the world," said Arthur Link, "to have had as its active, policy-making president, over a period of several crucial years, an educator who went on to become a national and world statesman and the architect of a new world order. What makes this more than merely an interesting statistic is that Woodrow Wilson was a creative philosopher and designer not only in world affairs but in higher education as well. He left a lasting mark on American colleges and universities generally, but especially on Princeton.

"Today's Princeton reflects Wilson almost perfectly. It's hard to believe: Everything he stood for is being vindicated and realized—the withering away of class privilege, which was never institutionalized here; his belief that fundamental human values must underlie everything; Princeton's openness, to people of all cultures, religions, races; and its commitment to the pursuit of truth.

"Partly because his influence was so broad, most of

Winner of the Bancroft Prize in 1957 and 1961 for two of his many biographical studies of Woodrow Wilson, Link has been a Princeton history professor since 1960 and director of the *Papers of Woodrow Wilson*, now at forty-nine volumes, scheduled to total sixty-three. With an A.B. and Ph.D. from the University of North Carolina, he has taught at Northwestern and at Oxford, which awarded him an M.A. He has been active in the national Presbyterian Church, and has been president of the Southern Historical Association, the American Historical Association, and the Organization of American Historians.

what can be said of Princeton can be said of other
universities of its type." But there are differences? He
nodded.

"One doesn't want to be invidious, but I believe that
among all major nonsectarian universities, Princeton is
the one that sustains most unabashedly the Jewish-
Christian tradition, its basic values and morals as
interpreted by Wilson, in this day of secularism, aliena-
tion, and cynicism." That was his conclusion, he said,
from looking closely at Princeton and similar institutions as a member of the Princeton Faculty Committee
on the Chapel, which conducted a year-long analysis
prior to the search for a new dean of the chapel which
ended in 1981 with the appointment of the Reverend
Frederick H. Borsch '57.

"To me personally, this was the most important
thing to come out of the search, and it supported my
feeling that Wilson's religious attitude is still alive at
Princeton." How would he describe that attitude? "To
Wilson, truth was a vital component of religion. He
believed anything true was 'from God.' Therefore a
religious person should never be afraid of the truth:
should not only accept it, but seek it, glorify it. To him,
scientific or scholarly research was a religious act; there
was no conflict between education and religion in his
mind as there was—and is—in some people's.

"This was in harmony with the Jewish traditional
belief in freedom of inquiry. Most fundamentalism, he
felt, was based on insecurity about religion; ner-
vousness and personal anxiety; a *fear* of God. Wilson's
faith was so strong that it could accommodate new
discoveries; celebrate them. The point is, Wilson
brought a religious zeal to his work as an educator, and
some of that persists at Princeton today, and helps to
characterize the place.

"There is something about having a man like Wilson
in an institution's history, in its bloodstream. Most of

us on the chapel committee felt this, I think; came to understand better his idea that education, knowledge, understanding were part of 'revelation' and, properly understood and put together, brought wholeness and spiritual health to a university; made it as religious a place as church, because both have the same objective: the search for truth, which is the word of God.

"I'd say that attitude is still alive at Princeton, though it's unconscious in the minds of a lot of people." As we walked out of Prospect, former home of Princeton presidents including Wilson, now a lunching and dinner-meeting place for faculty and administration, Link looked back and said, "You know, it's mind-blowing—a term I don't often use!—to think that from this house Wilson went on to a great place in history. Gives you a ghostly feeling!" And as we passed the chapel, with its niched sculpture of James McCosh, president during Wilson's undergraduate days: "Wilson almost worshiped, certainly idealized, McCosh. Both were nonfundamentalist Presbyterians to whom Christianity represented a great liberating force. Both blasted away at fundamentalism—but 'blast' is not the right word. They did it quietly and effectively. They had the same humanness and openness. And the university reflects them both.

"Wilson broke the hold of the fundamentalist Presbyterian heretic-hunters on the Princeton board of trustees, with help from other trustees and faculty members; opened things up, freed the faculty appointment process from the board's control, raised the intellectual standing of the place. He was building a first-rate faculty and laying the foundation for Princeton's preeminence in science. Many scholars he talked with said he had the keenest mind they had ever encountered, which was part of his ability to attract good people. One said, 'After talking with him for a half-hour, I would follow him anywhere.' He was instrumental in rescuing Princeton from mediocrity and transforming it into an incipient university. He kept it in the race at a crisis point, at a time when there was a popular saying that Harvard, with its system of electives, was 'dinner a la carte'; Yale, 'table d'hote'; Columbia, with its three-year degree program, 'a quick lunch'; and Princeton—'a picnic.'

"But after Wilson had raised academic admission standards, tightened discipline, and revised the under-graduate curriculum, it was said, 'Princeton used to be one of the easiest places to get into. Now it's one of the easiest to get out of.' Wilson took the view that 'I know better than any sophomore what sophomores should study,' an attitude that survives in Princeton's course requirements, independent work, and so on.

"By the time in 1905 when the trustees accepted his preceptorial plan, Wilson had already hired most of the new young faculty members, having personally inter-viewed—and, as many said, 'inspired' —them. What's sometimes lost sight of is that through this device he doubled the size of the faculty.

"He seemingly lost some big battles: to replace the exclusive eating clubs with 'colleges,' and to locate the Graduate College on the main campus. But he has won 'in the fullness of time,' an expression he liked to use, because those ideas, though buried, stayed alive in the institutional memory. Recurring pressure from stu-dents and faculty has changed the club system, opened it up, and given birth to a college system now being put in place; and the interaction he wanted between under-graduate and graduate students is taking place to some extent even though their residences are still separated by a brisk walk."

As we reached his door, Link looked back over the campus. "As Wilson said in his last baccalaureate ser-mon: 'There is a sense, a very real sense, not mystical but a plain fact of experience, in which the spirit of truth, of knowledge, of hope, of revelation, dwells in a place like this.'"

*"To me 'maturing' means
...learning to interact with
others as well as act alone—
and to enjoy doing it."*

15

EUGENE Y. LOWE, JR.

A s one person after another spoke of the close relationship that can exist between undergraduates and their professors at Princeton, in contrast to universities where the faculty is more remote, a question grew in my mind: Does this almost familial atmosphere tend to prolong students' adolescence, delay their maturing, leave them less fit at graduation time to face the "real" world?

Eugene Lowe seemed a good person to ask. He had experienced Princeton as an undergraduate in the class of 1971, as a university trustee for more than ten years, and was now back on campus as dean of students and a member of the faculty. He had a reputation for being a student of students.

He said my question was a reasonable one "provided it's understood that 'almost familial' does not mean Princeton professors play a soft, indulgent kind of parental role toward students. By being accessible they do show a parental concern and respect for their students, but they are far from being indulgent; in fact, as a group, they may be unusually demanding because, being personally acquainted with most of their stu-

---

An American church historian and Episcopal priest, Lowe, a member of Princeton's Class of 1971, holds graduate degrees in theology and history from Union Theological Seminary. He taught there and at General Theological Seminary and served on the staff of Calvary/St. George's Parish (New York City) before returning to Princeton in 1983 as dean of students and a member of the religion department.

dents, they are especially aware of their progress or lack of it. As to the effect of the atmosphere on students' maturation..."

He drew on a freshly lit pipe, looked from his West College office window across Cannon Green to the chapel tower visible back of East Pyne, and said, "Let me try an autobiographical approach to your question.

"When I was an undergraduate here, Professor John Wilson of the religion department was my academic adviser. It would be hard for me to describe how important he was in my life then—and still is! I don't believe I've made a single major vocational decision since I've known him—from undergraduate days right up to the present—without consulting him."

To suggest how deep the friendship with Wilson had been—"as student-faculty friendships often are here"— he elaborated on its continuation after graduation. "He was a trustee of Union Theological Seminary while I was a student there, and we often talked things over. Now he is my senior faculty colleague in the religion department and I'm the preceptor in two of his lecture courses. He's the master of Forbes College—formerly Princeton Inn—and I, as chairman of the Council of Masters, work closely with him and the other masters. Small point: I was in the first class of students to move into that college, and I think Wilson was my first faculty dinner guest.

"My relationship with John Wilson was probably especially intense because we were in the same field and because as a so-called 'University Scholar' I had an unusual amount of curricular flexibility and so a greater need for advice than most students have. But the fact is, all Princeton students have access to that kind of relationship with a professor. Even if they don't want it, this is simply not a place where a student can get into a position of isolation from the faculty; or not for long, anyway. There are too many built-in arrangements for drawing them together.

"Now, do such relationships prolong a student's adolescence? Did mine with John Wilson—and, on a lesser scale, with other professors and administrators—delay my maturing? Maybe I'm not the one to answer that!" A characteristic quick laugh, a pause. "It depends on how you define maturing. If it means learning to get along without other people, to be a loner in pursuit of knowledge and other goals—then no, I don't believe Princeton does encourage that as much as some of her sister institutions do, where the faculty is more aloof and students are more on their own.

"But to me that is *not* what the term means. To me 'maturing' means learning to get along and work with others, including some older and wiser than oneself, and different in other ways; learning to interact with others as well as act alone—and to enjoy doing it; to acknowledge and embrace interdependence.

"That kind of maturity is very much enhanced by the way students and professors interact at Princeton." To illustrate: "When I came back to Princeton to become dean of students, I might, in theory, have drawn into myself, called on my own observations and reflections to give me the ideas I needed. Instead, because of habits formed as an undergraduate, and principles learned, I sought out people to listen to, and drew on their experience. Alone, I was not at all sure of myself in this office, but in dialogue with my colleagues I could feel their wisdom and strength—and maturity—become a part of me."

He said it was, of course, common for especially gifted and aggressive students at other universities to establish close relations with professors in their fields, "but it's not the accepted thing to the degree it is here." He said he had heard more than one alumnus of other universities speak of the need to "break down doors" to get at senior professors.

The maturity-encouraging interaction between

Princeton students and faculty "takes place in a context of interaction that involves virtually everything this university does, beginning, on the academic level, with the preceptorial, which is symbol and essence of interaction; of Princeton's recognition that education is a very relational activity. Students bring their own experiences and outlooks to bear on the subject matter, make up their own minds; but they do it in interaction with a small group of fellow students and a faculty member. They're encouraged to put forth their own views, but to listen to others, too; *to put themselves in someone else's skin.* And you hear them saying of an argument opposed to their own, 'Hey! That may have possibilities.'

"I can't imagine an educational device better calculated to prepare students to deal in a mature way with today's world—whose problems call for working with people unlike oneself, listening to them, getting inside their skins."

His assistant put her head in: The student crisis that had seemed only threatening an hour ago had now materialized. He rose like a man accustomed to crises, and as we walked to the door I asked whether there was one word to express the institutional quality he had been describing.

"Collegiality: The belief that the kind of decisions one has to make in an educational institution—as in the world generally, nowadays—are most likely to be sound if the decision making involves a broad range of colleagues who know how to work together and are mature enough to enjoy doing it."

[Weeks after my talk with Lowe I came across the following lines by Christian Gauss, longtime dean of the college at Princeton: "The art of learning to live together and cooperate with each other is the most important of all the liberal arts."]

"Separating sheep from goats is very difficult in undergraduate years....So I was always slow in concluding who was and was not worth my time."

16

ALPHEUS T. MASON

"I never visited a college or university I didn't like, and I never taught a class I didn't enjoy," said Alpheus Mason. "And the similarities I observed are more significant than the differences."

But as a guest lecturer while still on the Princeton faculty, and later on his twelve-year round of postretirement visiting professorships, he noticed that "at other major universities I was an object of surprised attention—found myself a bit of a freak—simply because I treated students the way senior professors at Princeton generally treat their students; paid them a respect many had not felt from a professor before. At some sister institutions the faculty attitude toward undergraduates is almost contemptuous. At the end of my last class at one of these, a student asked if he could come to my room and talk. I said, 'Sure,' this being the kind of thing that happens all the time at Princeton. Leaving, after an hour's talk, the student said, 'Professor, you are

---

After teaching for forty-three years in Princeton's politics department, Mason retired in 1968 and in the next twelve years was a visiting professor at fifteen other colleges and universities, including Harvard, Yale, Dartmouth, Johns Hopkins, and the Universities of Virginia, California (Santa Barbara), Colorado, Michigan, and Minnesota. He earned his A.B. at Dickinson College, Ph.D. at Princeton, and taught at Trinity College (now Duke University) before joining the Princeton faculty. He has published more than twenty scholarly books including best-selling biographies of U.S. Supreme Court justices Brandeis, Stone, and Taft.

the first faculty member of rank I've talked with like this in my four years here.' What was routine at Princeton was apparently unusual there."

Such experiences "pointed up for me Princeton's differentness in its attitude toward undergraduates. There is a tradition, here, of appreciating each as an individual; of helping each to find him- —and now her- —self." Helping them how? "Basically, simply by respecting them; which makes enormous sense, because no one knows what the potential of a given student is at that age and stage.

"Separating sheep from goats is very difficult in undergraduate years. Sometimes a student who doesn't seem like much at first will just grow like a weed if you challenge and encourage him. Another, who seems very bright, of whom he and everyone else expects great things, will peter out. So I was always slow in concluding who was and was not worth my time. You never knew when a spark would flare." And that attitude, he said, prevails at Princeton.

"There's a humanness about the place. The high ratio of faculty to students makes it possible for professors to spend time with students, but the impetus actually to do this comes from the University's philosophy."

Which is—?

"That students and teachers should educate each other. It's the opposite of the monologue method, where you stand up and tell students what you know, which is like trying to teach somebody to ride a bicycle by riding it yourself and letting them watch you. No, you have to let the student get on the bicycle, and fall off, and perhaps even get hurt a little.

"It's the Socratic method: raising questions, letting students find, or try to find, the answers. And one thing they learn is, the best questions can't be fully and finally answered. The greatest thinkers—and teachers—are not the ones who answer questions but who raise them; and who encourage students to raise them. In my life I've made a close study and analysis of the classics. Do you know why they endure? Because they ask questions that are baffling—and often unanswerable."

He said Princeton's approach to teaching goes back even farther, "but the real revolution came in 1905 when Woodrow Wilson brought in fifty young professors as 'preceptors.' This sudden infusion of talent, dedicated to a certain type of small-group teaching, was strongly and immediately felt—and is still being felt, passed on from generation to generation. Its influence may be inexhaustible."

Instead of departing from it in later years, Princeton supplemented it with—for seniors—the four-course plan and the senior thesis, and with a general emphasis on independent work. "It was Wilson's notion that each teacher should be 'philosopher, guide, and friend' to his students. This had been the attitude at Princeton all along. It was at most American colleges in the early days, but Wilson institutionalized it at Princeton." Might it have survived without that? "It didn't elsewhere."

Many times voted Princeton's "most inspiring teacher," Mason volunteered that he had been "something of a prima donna," and that this was not unusual among his fellow professors: "to love the plaudits of undergraduates." I asked him to define "prima donna," which to me implied egotism and a difficult temperament. "No," he said. "To me it means a fella who for whatever reason stands out in the eyes of his public. And I made an effort to stand out! So did some others. In my early years, Princeton had a lot of prima donnas, and still has. 'Buzzer' Hall was a prime example, with the bulldog he brought to class with him, and his neckties, which seniors, singing on the steps of Nassau Hall, said 'were made of Garibaldi's underwear.'"

He said the principle of dynamic interplay between teacher and student can be—and at Princeton usually is—applied even in large lecture courses, where "a professor has the choice of simply pouring out his knowledge without concern for how it will go down with students, or of planning his remarks with some respect for students' curiosity; trying to figure out what questions will be aroused in students' minds by each statement, and organizing his material to be responsive.

"The best teachers have a gift for giving: an urge as irresistible as the artist's. Human beings are the teacher's material as surely as paint is the painter's. A teacher's goal should not be to fill out his own self-image but to help others discover and discipline and develop their own God-given talents.

"Princeton has no monopoly on outstanding teachers, but thanks to Wilson and others, a method of teaching is standard here to a greater degree than at larger universities. There is more opportunity here for contact among professors: more cross-fertilization."

Would he agree with those who say Princeton works its students uncommonly hard?

"You bet! Undergraduate *and* graduate students." He said seventeen students turned up for the first meeting of his graduate seminar on American Political Thought at a leading Ivy League university. "When I announced that I would expect each to write a paper a week—as had been my custom at Princeton—the seventeen then and there dropped to three! They just refused to do that much work!" He quoted from John Stuart Mill's autobiography: "A student of whom nothing is asked that he cannot do never does all he can."

One conspicuous way Princeton demonstrates its respect for undergraduates, he said, is in having them taught by the same professors who teach graduate students (the "single-faculty" system), whereas at some comparable universities undergraduates are taught

mainly by graduate students and new Ph.D.s and seldom see the senior faculty.

How significant is this, educationally?

"Very." Why? "The senior faculty member is, obviously, a scholar—or a scientist deeply involved in
research. Unlike the graduate student or the freshly
minted Ph.D., he has been pushing at the frontiers of
knowledge in his field for some time, and not merely
reading of those who have done this. The odd thing is,
this can make for a kind of modesty: He knows better
what he doesn't know! And it can make him more
patient with undergraduates, more sensitive to un-
answered questions than the younger scholar who, in
earning his Ph.D., has just found the answer to one big
question and tends to be more preoccupied with answers than questions."

Both graduate and undergraduate students profit
from the single-faculty system, he said. "The custom of
using original sources with graduate students carries
over to undergraduate teaching and puts it on a higher
plane. The effort needed to make such material more
accessible to undergraduates can carry over to graduate
teaching and make it livelier. Undergraduates at places
like Princeton, because of their youth and exceptional
brightness and openness, are very inspiring to teach,
and graduate students benefit from teaching thus
inspired."

If the Princeton method is so good, why don't all
institutions adopt it?

"Well, let's face it: The Princeton method is damned
expensive!"

But other institutions are as rich as Princeton or
richer—?

"Yes, but they're not spending their money that way!
Their primary interest is research, and undergraduates
are sometimes seen as a necessary nuisance; whereas
Princeton has retained, from its early days, the notion

that teaching ranks with research as an activity demanding and deserving the very best talents, even of
scholars working toward the discovery of important
new knowledge."

In his postretirement teaching travels, he was struck
by the sharp distinction drawn elsewhere between
scholarship/research and teaching, "as if there were a
contradiction between the two; and when one has to be
sacrificed or downgraded, it has to be teaching. Well,
it's obviously possible for a very good scientist or scholar
to be so absorbed in research that he has tunnel vision, is
distracted by teaching. I know such people exist. But
I—and Princeton professors generally—found it not
only possible but necessary to combine the two. I
believe that to be a good teacher you have to be
continually pushing back the frontiers of learning,
through research. You can't be forever taking in other
people's intellectual wash and be a successful teacher.
But it's hard for me to understand how a person
working at the frontiers of some subject can fail to be
helpfully stimulated by the sheer fun of working with
young people just entering that field!

"In my own case, I've rarely given an undergraduate
lecture that didn't find its way into an article or book. I
always wrote out my lectures, didn't talk off the top of
my head. I know these lectures were enriched and
influenced—as was the research that went into them—
by my awareness that they would be delivered to an
audience of live bodies. It kept me from developing a
textbookish style." He paused. "Hell, a good many of
my books would never have been written if I hadn't had
an undergraduate audience to write them for in the first
place!"

From a bookcase filled with his own published works
he took *Security through Freedom* and showed me its
table of contents. "Every single chapter originated as a
lecture to undergraduates!" Next he showed me the

preface to his biography of Justice Harlan Stone, in which he acknowledged help from two undergraduate "fellow researchers" whose digging for their senior theses turned up material he could use. "Many universities fail to appreciate the creative capacities of undergraduates—in all fields."

Another reason more universities do not adopt the Princeton method, he said, is that not all professors are equipped, emotionally or intellectually, to use it. "Most teachers talk too much, which the Princeton method discourages. Some students used to criticize me for letting *them* talk so much. 'We'd rather hear what *you* have to say.' I explained that I wanted them to become involved. It takes patience."

What else?

"Deep self-assurance; confidence that you can relax your control over students and yet get it back when you need to, if things start to get out of hand. You need to know *people* and not just an academic subject. You have to know how to let a student know, without insulting him, that he's being boring and tedious and wasting everybody's time, including his own."

Would he as a keen observer of current public affairs say the "Princeton method" has any special relevance today? He said his answer would be oblique.

"When I came here, the tradition in teaching graduate seminars was to assign readings and one long research paper each semester. But this seemed boring to me as a teacher. I wanted more interaction. So I devised a system nobody else was using: There would be a body of reading all students would do, and then, each week, each student would submit a 'query' on the material; a question it raised in his mind. Then each student would choose one of those queries and write a short documented research paper on it each week. Now what was the virtue of that approach? It encouraged students not simply to seek answers but to seek questions, which takes some humility.

"This approach is just heaven-sent today, when our problems—energy, defense, the economy—are so numerous and complex that no one has convincing answers to any of them. There never was a time when we so needed to break our problems down into queries, and research each one, finding a few answers and a lot more questions."

"I feel my research is improved by my teaching, by the prodding I get from inquiring young minds of high caliber." 17

ROBERT M. MAY

He has the lean, expressive face and body of a Marcel Marceau, and when Robert May feels enthusiasm for a subject, he projects it—to the back of a crowded lecture hall or across a lunch table.

His enthusiasm on this occasion was for the "sponsored" research done by all leading American universities, which he felt deserved the continued support of government agencies, private industry, and foundations.

He was less disposed to describe how universities differ in their approach to research; but, prodded, acknowledged that such differences do exist and help define each institution's character.

"I would not go so far as to call Princeton unique with respect to research," he said, "but it is at one end of a continuum of the fifty or so top American universities." Which end? "Princeton has a clear view, deliberately formed over many years, of the kind of university it wants to be: A place committed to excellence in research *and* to the integration of that research—and

---

After earning his B.Sc. and Ph.D. from Sydney University in his native Australia, May taught applied mathematics at Harvard and physics at Sydney before coming to Princeton to teach biology. His present research deals especially with the role of infectious diseases in the regulation of natural populations of plants and animals. He is author of *Stability and Complexity in Model Ecosystems* and of *Theoretical Ecology: Principles and Applications,* and is also editor of the series Princeton Monographs on Population Biology. He is a Fellow of the Royal Society and the American Academy of Arts and Sciences.

90

the men and women who conduct it—into the educational fabric of the university. It does not seek or accept outside grants for sponsored research that might distort that commitment."

And at the opposite end of the continuum—?

"Those universities that allow or encourage their professional schools and departments to become free-standing empires bringing in huge research grants almost regardless of the shape—or shapelessness—the resulting activities will give to the institutions. Some people call these 'multiversities.' It must be emphasized, though, that they do extremely important work.

"At Princeton, scientific and scholarly research not only has to be carried out within a regular department of the university but has to be clearly related to that department's academic program. And the scientists and scholars conducting the research are expected to teach—not only graduate and postdoctoral students but undergraduates. Some other private universities have similar policies, but probably not as clearly articulated or as closely observed.

"At very large public universities, and even at some of the larger private ones, there are faculty 'superstars' who are allowed to concentrate on their own research and stay away from students; who cower at the prospect of facing a freshman. At Princeton, senior and junior professors are treated more nearly as equals, and this creates an atmosphere of collegiality. We are not divided, as some are, into superstars reigning in islands of excellence, and a sea of drudges around them doing the teaching. I'm not saying our system is all good and theirs is all bad; they produce some brilliant work. I happen to prefer the atmosphere at Princeton, but that's largely personal."

Why does he prefer it?

"I feel my research is improved by my teaching, by the prodding I get from inquiring young minds of high caliber to look at things in my field in a new way. And whereas many—maybe most—scientists don't like being involved in university administration, I find it stimulating to move from one world to another: from research, to teaching, to administration.

"I like to see how things work; and to affect how they work. Princeton, while large enough to provide me with the graduate students, facilities, and financial support I need for my research, is small enough for me to comprehend. The other universities I know best, Oxford and Cambridge, although fragmented into individual colleges that are significantly smaller than Princeton, are so administratively complex that I doubt if any mortal fully understands them. And Imperial College, in London, where I spend my summers, and Harvard, where I have taught, also appear to me to have overall administrations that—because of their size—are too complex for anyone but a full-time administrator to grasp. I'm told this is true of most American universities, encrusted as they are with professional schools."

May does indeed affect how things work at Princeton. He is chairman of the University Research Board (URB), which oversees the seeking and accepting of outside funds for scientific and scholarly research; and ranking as an academic dean, he sits with the provost and the deans of the faculty, of the college, and of the Graduate School in making crucial decisions on matters far removed from sponsored research, including the undergraduate curriculum, student aid, student life, and support of graduate students.

Is Princeton's URB significantly different from comparable bodies at other universities?

"Somewhat different from those at other private universities, vastly different from those at vaster institutions."

Different how?

"Historically, Princeton recognized earlier than most universities the need for faculty oversight of the acceptance of outside funds for research. In the post-Sputnik 1950s, when such funds were beginning to be available on a large scale, we happened to have, in Henry DeWolf Smyth '18 and Sir Hugh Taylor, two faculty members who had had extensive experience in working as scientists on the Manhattan Project during World War II, and, as university people, in working with government bodies after the war. They had definite ideas of what should and should not happen in the inevitable evolution of these government-university relationships. They wanted them to evolve in a coherent way, and not just existentially as they were beginning to do at other universities.

"So Princeton has been prepared for thirty years to deal with the questions that are now confronting universities as a result of research into recombinant DNA and other matters with complex public-ethical-commercial implications. Already set up to think about these questions, we have done so with little fuss.

"As to its functioning, the Princeton research board is somewhat unusual in that every proposal by a faculty member seeking outside funding for research is looked at by two of the six faculty members of the board [there are also three administrators, and the chairman], not as a 'peer review' but to see whether it is consistent with university policies, which are broadly drawn but include these points:

"One, no 'classified' research; nothing not freely accessible to the public. Most universities have such a policy now, but Princeton has had it for years.

"Two, research must be fundamentally integrated into the teaching of undergraduate and graduate students, not aimed solely or primarily at developing or improving products for their own sake. We discourage the creation of those free-standing empires whose main virtue, often, is that they bring in money. We don't say, as some do, 'This money is available from an outside source: What can you work up in the way of a proposal to get it?' We say, 'What do you want to do? Lay it out and we'll try to find support for it.'"

He said it was probably worth mentioning that "the chairmanship of similar boards elsewhere is usually, necessarily, a full-time job. Here, the chairman is expected to go on teaching at all levels, and doing research. This is possible because of Princeton's size.

"Although sponsored research at Princeton—excluding the Plasma Physics Laboratory out on Route 1, which is the center of the U.S. fusion research effort—brings in some thirty million dollars annually through some seven hundred separate grants and contracts, Princeton remains a small-scale enterprise in comparison with places like Michigan or Berkeley. Chairmanship of the URB at Princeton is compatible with being productive in one's own research, and with teaching. A succession of chairmen—from Smyth and Taylor in early days to Lyman Spitzer and Sheldon Judson '40 before me—testify to this."

Is it advantageous to have a working faculty member preside over the board that sets and monitors research policy for other faculty members?

"Yes. A line is not drawn between 'them,' the administration, and 'us,' the faculty, as it tends to be elsewhere. Things are done with greater understanding and civility when you don't view a dispute—and there are bound to be some in this work—as a Manichean dichotomy. The atmosphere is different. It's partly the size of the place, of course; you're less likely to get confrontational with a colleague you may be playing tennis with the next day."

Did he agree with those who say Princeton characteristically tends more toward theoretical research than its opposite?

As he mulled over the question, I reflected that he is a prime specimen of the theoretical scientist. He gave up theoretical physics a decade ago to apply the mathematical techniques of that field to ecology and evolutionary biology, which he has helped to revolutionize. He studies nature abstractly, mathematically, seeking patterns in the data collected by empirical ecologists; patterns on which to base predictions of the dynamic behavior of populations of organisms from blue whales to epidemic viruses.

"Yes," he said, "it's probably fair to say Princeton has been especially drawn to theoretical research through the years, partly because of its size: You don't need large groups of people or large pieces of machinery or a large and costly administrative infrastructure to support theoretical research.

"However, Princeton has long recognized the danger of letting the theoretical dominate; the danger that you may end up with a sort of Brahmin institution that attracts people who don't want to get their hands dirty; who have the Aristotelian attitude that all problems can be solved just by thinking about them.

"Aware that a university, to be first-rate, needs to have a blend of the theoretical and the empirical—with all the laboratory work, the mess, and great and increasing expense it entails—Princeton has devised an effective strategy for achieving this blend. It is a continuing struggle, involving not only Princeton's concept of itself but the deployment of funds."

In pursuit of this goal, May has been active at every stage in the planning of Princeton's new molecular biology department—"especially," with a wry smile, "in insisting it would cost a lot more than was at first thought"—and he believes its presence on campus will weigh significantly on the empirical side of keeping Princeton in balance as a research university.

"Not to end on a negative note," he said as we left the lunch table at Prospect, "but there are some hard, almost cruel, aspects to being a small university with high aspirations. One, only a small fraction of assistant professors make it into tenure here; some who don't make it are very able people, respected and liked, who like it here but have to move on simply because there isn't room for them to move up. Two, in a place as small as this there are certain diseconomies of scale, one effect of which, on scientists, is that to sustain a research enterprise at a given level of funding, to be competitive with larger institutions, you have to work harder here!"

He smiled and hurried back to work.

"The physical beauty of the place, in combination with its history, reflects accurately and harmoniously what the institution is all about."

18

NEIL L. RUDENSTINE

"Princeton has a particularly clear 'presence,'" said Neil Rudenstine, "one that demands a personal response from students. While not the whole story, the beauty of the campus contributes to this 'presence.'

"Princeton was the first university I visited as a prospective student, and, fresh from reading *This Side of Paradise,* I fell in love at first sight. It was a dazzling spring day, and though I would be struck later that year by the attractiveness of other campuses, especially Harvard and Amherst, they didn't remove the spell of Princeton: its stunning beauty, the whole sense of quintessential college life.

"I still remember, vividly, spring evenings of my freshman year, the lights shining in the darkness..." He shook his head. "There is something about the sweep and scale of Princeton, its architecture, the number of vistas. They make indelible prints on the consciousness—especially of undergraduates. And the phys-

---

After graduation from Princeton in 1956, Rudenstine went to Oxford as a Rhodes Scholar for another A.B.; then, having been in the ROTC program at Princeton, he served as an army first lieutenant at Ft. Sill, Oklahoma, before earning his Ph.D. at Harvard, where he taught for four years. He returned to Princeton as English professor and dean of student affairs in the troublous late 1960s, later became dean of the college, and at the time of this conversation was provost. His academic field is Renaissance literature.

ical beauty of the place, in combination with its history, reflects accurately and harmoniously what the institution is all about.

"Princeton wouldn't have the emanations it has without two and a half centuries behind it: the history that's taken place here, and the concept of the university sustained throughout all that. So the physical image has depth: Princeton is weathered and strengthened by the past. This, with one's personal experience of the place, helps to account for the warm loyalty of many alumni. Even if their ties are suspended or broken in the years just after graduation, the experience and image are potent enough to resurface."

Does Princeton's "presence" relate significantly to its ability to educate students?

"Very much so. It means the air students breathe here—the institutional atmosphere—has a 'charge' to it. The visible and historical presence really forces every student to come to terms with the university, one way or another. At some universities the institutional presence is neutralized by its surrounding environment, especially in a large city; at others, by the number of 'colleges' and 'schools' and the way they are spread over a large area. It can be hard to come to terms with such institutions.

"Princeton's presence is formidable and inescapable. From the beginning, you powerfully identify with it or resist it, love it or hate it; you can't ignore it. This is one source of Princeton's energy, and of its ability to communicate its energy: the way it refuses to take 'No' for an answer. Even if you don't like it, you have to end up with a positive feeling for what human attention, care, and loving concern have created over many generations. The residential nature of the university, the total environment—there is no alternative to finding one's place in it. And yet it is open enough, large enough, varied enough not to be felt as constricting. It is now, after all, a community of some ten thousand people, students, faculty, and staff."

Had his being an English major perhaps made him unusually sensitive to the Princeton "presence"? "No. I had friends in many other fields, and roomed with two engineering students during most of my undergraduate years. Most had very similar responses."

Many other elements contribute to the strength of alumni feelings, he said, including "a disproportionately large number of unifying rituals at Princeton: things an entire class goes through as grueling experiences on the way to a goal, particularly the junior paper and senior thesis. Students also share a ritualistic context within which work is done: the honor code, preceptorials, the library, the relationship between faculty and students."

Is there a type of student for whom Princeton is particularly appropriate?

He prefaced his "Yes" by saying "there is more elbow room for diversity at Princeton today than ever before, making it hospitable and attractive to students from a wide variety of regional, ethnic, social, and economic backgrounds, with widely divergent talents and interests. This diversity is crucial to maintaining educational quality. At the same time, there *are* probably some characteristics shared by a great many of our undergraduates. I believe most want to *participate in* an institution. Princeton invites this, saying, in conscious and unconscious ways, 'We want you to identify with this place, care about it, help shape it.' This gets communicated by our Alumni Schools Committee members in interviewing applicants; by the faculty in the clear way they commit themselves to so many aspects of undergraduate education; by the way the university describes itself in its literature. We stress, probably more than most institutions of our kind, the possibilities and advantages of an association that can last a lifetime.

"So—granting the elbow room for diversity—a great many of our students probably tend to be unusually public-spirited and service-minded; they want to participate fully in this or any other institution they join. Not all of them, of course; and there are, fortunately, many different ways in which one can serve. But whether it's the spirit of James Madison, Woodrow Wilson, or Adlai Stevenson, it's very powerful. You see it in applications for admission, where students discuss their goals in life, and the kinds of activities they wish to be involved in."

Is there a type of student for whom Princeton is *not* ideal?

"I'd hate to divide all humankind into categories on this issue! And I believe virtually any talented, thoughtful young person can have a rewarding time at Princeton. But perhaps the alternative to the attitude I've been describing could be called 'instrumental'; that is, the feeling that a college is mainly a resource one 'uses'—and I don't mean that term in a pejorative sense: a place you want to go through and out of, not feeling you've entered a precinct that you will always, in some sense, remain in, and that will always remain in you. Princeton invites a more lasting connection."

As provost, Rudenstine has special responsibility for the university's budget, and thus for determining priorities. Does a small university need to pay more attention to "priorities" than a larger one?

"Yes. Here, there is constantly the question of choice, the need to select: 'Do we want this—*or* that?' At larger places there may be a tendency to think, 'Maybe we can have this *and* that.' Princeton has about the smallest faculty that could successfully mount major programs on both the undergraduate and graduate levels. We're

really just at the 'critical mass' size, where every single faculty member and every course simply has to count. This makes for a highly disciplined curriculum."
But less flexibility?
"Yes, to some extent. But that question should be looked at in the context of particular historical eras. There are times when it may be appropriate to place a special premium on flexibility and adventurousness in academic fields because the society may be suffering from a lack of these things. There are other times when society, in its desire for flexibility, loses some of its ability to distinguish between what is really fundamental, important knowledge and what is ephemeral. In such times, the need in universities will almost certainly be for structures that force a careful evaluation of alternatives, a concentration on absolutely central academic and other values.

"My own feeling is that this is, and has been for some time, and will be for some years to come, nationally and internationally, the latter kind of period, when the great need is for intelligent selection and focus. A number of institutions have been injured by too much flexibility. We see some evidence of this in current efforts across the country to eliminate some of the things added in the last fifteen to twenty years, to return to a 'core.' Princeton, because its intrinsic structure is not unsuited to difficult times, may in the end be in a better position than most to sustain intelligent selectivity and genuine flexibility."

"The senior thesis makes you do the kind of original work that makes you feel you're an original human being."

19

CARL E. SCHORSKE

During his "first teaching stand" at Wesleyan University in Connecticut, Carl Schorske spent a leave of absence at the Center for Advanced Study in the Behavioral Sciences at Palo Alto. He guest-lectured at nearby Berkeley and was invited to join its history faculty.

"On that visit I was exhilarated by the large, responsive student audience. Immediately I got the feel of a big urban university, impersonal yet pulsating, far removed from my previous experience. And after fourteen years at Wesleyan, though I loved it, I felt I should leave it, and not become an elder statesman too early! So I took Berkeley's offer.

"Berkeley gave me my first exposure to graduate students in a serious way. I liked that, and liked the big lecture courses; but I missed the personal contact I'd had with undergraduates at Wesleyan, my main contacts at Berkeley being with graduate students and faculty. Those undergraduates I did know at Berkeley seemed unusually mature for their age, having come, many of them, from a wide variety of social subgroups in large cities. They hadn't been protected from the maturing

---

Now Dayton-Stockton Professor of History, Emeritus, Schorske came to the Princeton faculty in 1969 with a Columbia A.B., a Harvard Ph.D., and having taught at Wesleyan (1946–60) and Berkeley (1960–69). He is known as a multidisciplinary scholar and has taught and written on a wide range of subjects from German politics to urban development. His *Fin-de-siècle Vienna* won a Pulitzer Prize in 1981, and the same year he received a five-year MacArthur Foundation Award.

effects of the outside world as had most of my students at Wesleyan—and, later, those I would teach at Princeton. It was more like a European university."

During the 1960s, he was in the middle of the "Free Speech" movement at Berkeley, which he said was much misunderstood. "It began not over the freedom to use dirty words, as was widely thought, but over the right of students to invite persons of any political persuasion to speak on the campus and to carry on political activity. I was instrumental in getting the rules changed to permit that, having been involved in the civil liberties movement for many years."

Berkeley fascinated him. "Public life in all forms was represented: from agribusiness to racial minority agitation: all the politics of California were refracted and intellectualized. It provided a link between public life and academic life, something this country very much needs; something deep in our tradition but now at a very low ebb. As an Enlightenment society, we've always believed in it; but it's been a parlous, fragile relationship, with, at one end, scholars tending to become totally abstract or merely neutral experts, and, at the other end, the public or the state often moving in and becoming destructive of the truth-seeking responsibilities a university is charged with when social interests are involved.

"California is the U.S. writ small, and Berkeley is California writ small. I've always been intrigued by 'places' —cities, villages, universities; always enjoyed getting familiar with some new corner of the U.S. or Europe; whenever I travel, I look for someone who can take me around, show me inside."

So he enjoyed Berkeley, but "became *too* involved in campus affairs," serving for a time as assistant to the chancellor for educational development, and felt his scholarship was suffering. He accepted an invitation to the Institute for Advanced Study in Princeton, and while there guest-lectured at the university, "liked what I saw, and said 'Yes' when asked to join the faculty.

"But leaving Berkeley was hard. When one lives through troubles one makes fast friends. There were people there I loved—and not always the ones I agreed with! The wonderful thing about the history department there: We provided the leaders for all factions, at both faculty and student levels. But when we met on departmental business we made our decisions along quite different lines: someone politically far left would be aligned with a person on the far right when it came to academic policy. This was exemplary and heartening; and not true to the same degree in other departments.

"Princeton, being middle sized, with very strong undergraduate teaching supported by the whole faculty, is more like Wesleyan; but it is like Berkeley in having an important graduate program as well, a strong scholarship-and-research commitment and orientation. It put the two pieces of my life together.

"I was very much impressed, while at the institute here, with the way President Goheen responded to the first tremors of student unrest. So far as I know, Princeton was the only major university—besides Chicago—that didn't say, 'It can't happen here.' Goheen recognized it *could* happen and went out to meet it.

"Princeton's performance in those times was 'in character' —and therefore says something about its character. The Princeton administration, though constructed on a centralized executive model, characteristically proceeds—with the utmost sensitiveness— to consult the feelings of community members, especially the faculty, before making a significant decision. It's the custom here to 'touch all bases.' When I was trying to help establish the European cultural studies program [at which he was ultimately successful], I became impatient with all the touching of bases—and, sure enough, the effort failed the first time around because all bases had *not* been touched.

"What Princeton has is a kind of administrative autocracy which relates itself to the opinions of crucial opinion-making sectors of the campus, particularly faculty and alumni. It's a system that doesn't allow the opening of fissures in the body politic, and works by addressing issues before they arise, prophylactically. It's characterized by the very great skill with which the administration gives most individuals the feeling they have been consulted.

"There are tremendous advantages to this system when it comes to riding out storms; but in some ways, the absence of open debate reduces the kind of tensions an institution can tolerate and probably needs. All the base-touching tends to inhibit, or mute, not only opposition but also public debate. Princeton has had a low tolerance for tension; a tendency to be better academically than intellectually."

Moving to Princeton's undergraduate program, Schorske praised the senior thesis as "the crown of independent work: the point at which Princeton's commitment to both education and research is most evident. Other universities have something similar, but only for honors students.

"As a student here you win your maturity by doing what scholars do: You pose new questions and damn well get the answers yourself. The students know, when they come here, a senior thesis will be demanded of them, and it infects most students with a healthy anxiety from the start. When meeting with alumni, older ones especially, I find the first thing they want to talk about is the great lecturers of the past; the second is the senior thesis. Ask where they think they learned the most and inevitably the answer is, 'the thesis.' Ask how they liked it, and they almost always say, 'I damn near died!' But that's where they *learned*."

I had been told he was a great lecturer, had received a rare standing ovation from students at his last lecture before retiring in 1980. "No, I'm not a *great* lecturer.

I'm a *good* one, though! The great ones of the old school carefully prepared their lecture texts in advance and delivered them for rhetorical effect as well as substance. My style is spontaneous—which takes enormous energy: You have to be like a tensile spring. But by thus doing your thinking out loud you demonstrate the process by which one *gets* learning."

The test of a good teacher, he said, is, "Do you regard 'learning' as a noun or a verb? If as a noun, as a thing to be possessed and passed along, then you present your truths, neatly packaged, to your students. But if you see 'learning' as a verb!—the process is different. The good teacher has learning, but tries to instill in students the desire to learn, and demonstrates the ways one goes about 'learning.'"

The senior thesis is one such way. "Students are encouraged to go out and interview authorities in a field, go to original sources. Many of my students were helped by Princeton to go to foreign countries where they got a sense of what it is to use an archive. The thesis makes you do the kind of original work that makes you feel you're an original human being!"

Is Princeton, because of its size, more hospitable to interdisciplinary teaching than larger universities?

"From the faculty point of view, yes. Elsewhere the departments are so strong, the walls separating one from another are so hard to breach. Here you have the walls, all right—Princeton is extremely conventional in its departmentalization—but you also have a capacity for breaching them." Musing on the interdisciplinary, Schorske said, "research people often live on the margins of their fields. Biochemistry is born when somebody in biology can't get a problem solved without chemistry; demography comes out of the interaction of statistics and genetics."

One of his particular interests is "where the margins of a discipline are: those peripheral areas celebrated in research but resisted by institutional structures, one trying to break out, the other trying to hold them in. If you have a good research faculty, you have people who are willing to mix it up. If you have a faculty committed to teaching, they *want* to mix it up. And students benefit from the mixing."

On balance, however, he thought Princeton not an easy place in which to implant interdisciplinary programs. "Princeton is rule-bound; the administration—and especially the faculty—is 'from Missouri': has to be *shown;* is not libertarian. But if you mobilize your evidence, you *can* move it. In some ways I regret Princeton's conservatism as to structure. You have to be extremely persistent to set up anything new. But if it's too tight here, it's too loose at other places. Here you have to show cause why something should be done: put up or shut up. I think there are times when the burden of proof should *not* be on the innovator. Here innovation has to follow demonstration. But—," he shrugged philosophically, "that's where you get your muscle."

"New scientific discoveries...can profoundly affect...how the human race will evolve. No one wants such power in the hands of men and women insensitive to the human dimension of what they're doing."

20

WILLIAM R. SCHOWALTER

"The scientist at Princeton," said William Schowalter, "is 'broadened' by having to come up against undergraduates.

"Most scientists, to further their careers, have to know precious little about anything not immediately related to their current research. A scientist doesn't have to know about, say, the latest Mideast crisis or trends in the modern novel to determine whether certain gas molecules colliding with a catalyst surface are going to sit on it right-side up, upside-down, sideways, or not at all"—an example that came to mind, he said, from his interest in current experiments to find practical uses for the otherwise noxious waste products of oil refineries.

"In science, anything done in a field other than your own, or even in your own more than two years earlier, may seem virtually irrelevant—on the surface. Even if

Theoretical and experimental aspects of fluid mechanics are the special interests of chemical engineer Schowalter, who earned his B.S. at the University of Wisconsin and his Ph.D. at the University of Illinois. He is the author of *Mechanics of Non-Newtonian Fluids,* has been a Sherman Fairchild Distinguished Scholar at California Institute of Technology, and a Senior Fellow of the British Science Research Council at the University of Cambridge. He is on visiting committees at Cornell, Lehigh, and MIT, and the editorial boards of several scholarly journals. He is a member of the National Academy of Engineering.

the world is falling apart around you, you can go on with your work and say, 'Don't bother me.'

"But it's hard to maintain that kind of single-minded concentration on your own specialty if you teach undergraduates, particularly the kind we get at Princeton. At some universities the undergraduates in science and engineering are almost preprofessional, locked into their future careers the way graduate students are, and they don't demand that their science professors be very broadly educated or interested.

"But at Princeton many students of the sciences are also very much interested in history, economics, literature, politics. When I was doing a lot of freshman advising for the engineering school I often heard students say they could have gone to some other distinguished school, 'but I came to Princeton because I wasn't sure I wanted to be an engineer.' About 40 to 45 percent of our engineering school undergraduates don't go into professional engineering but into medicine, law, or business.

"I think it's fair to say the average undergraduate a scientist deals with here is very different from the average nationwide. We simply don't get many who dutifully copy down what you say without questioning it. Our students are broadly curious and try to fit what you're saying into a broader context—and they press you to do that, too. And given the small class size Princeton strives to maintain, and the individual student counseling professors do here, you feel that pressure! That's what many of us find stimulating. I find it comfortable, too, to be in an environment where you can teach your own discipline with enthusiasm knowing your students are being exposed with equal enthusiasm to other disciplines."

The common notion that scientists dislike teaching undergraduates is contradicted by what Schowalter has observed at Princeton. "Some young faculty members come in with lukewarm feelings about having to teach so much, but get caught up in it, have ideas for new courses, and we have to tell them, 'You're teaching too much. Whether you get tenure here is going to depend on your research as well as your teaching, so don't get carried away with teaching.'"

It is not the contact with students, alone, that encourages breadth of mind in the scientist at Princeton, he said. "There are also the unusually, if not uniquely, close and amiable relationships that exist here between faculty and administration, and among professors of different disciplines. A scientist is much more likely here than at other research universities to sit on important committees with professors from a wide variety of other disciplines, including the humanities; to sit beside them in monthly faculty meetings and to have other professional and personal relationships with them in this relatively small, close-knit community."

Schowalter at the time of our talk was serving his fifth one-year term as a faculty-elected member of the committee that reviews all faculty appointments, advancements, and salary changes. "When I first heard of this committee I couldn't believe it made sense. How in the world could someone whose field is religion participate in the choice of a chemical engineering professor? But I've seen how similar the marks of superiority are in scholars from very different fields, and how much people of good will, working together, can contribute to good decisions.

"You learn to appreciate the insights differently trained minds, from widely different backgrounds, can bring to bear on the same problem. At Princeton we operate in what could be called 'a constructively resonated mode.' You're always saying to yourself, when someone makes a point, 'Aha! I hadn't thought of that!'"

Had he observed a lack of this sort of collaboration at other universities?

"Yes—and I've noticed it affects people in one of two ways: Some narrow specialists conclude they're superior because they don't have to waste time working with people outside their own specialties; others tend to feel inferior, or guilty, because they feel they *ought* to be more involved with matters and persons outside their fields."

As to wasted time, he said that if undergraduate teaching takes time away from research at Princeton, this is partially offset by the university's "efficient, time-saving support structure," and the absence of a "we-they" mentality between faculty and administration. "Professors from larger universities say they're amazed at how fast things get done here. One reason is that when you talk with a senior academic administrator here, you're talking with a fellow faculty member, and not, as at most places, with a professional administrator.

"At those larger universities, people tend pretty early in their careers to move into academic administration and become professionals at it. As a rule, the larger and more professional the bureaucracy, the longer it takes to get decisions and the less likely you are to be happy with the ones you get. Our deans seem to feel they are here to serve the faculty and not to protect their own turf; they still have one foot in teaching. Elsewhere the deans have come up from the trenches, all right, but their administrative duties are so time-consuming they tend to forget what the university's purpose is."

Going back to his earlier point about the scientist's tendency to develop tunnel vision: How important is this?

"Very. It's not new, but is becoming more important. But before going into that, let me say that if you take scientists who are well known in their fields, nationally or internationally, they are probably more broadly educated and informed than the average nonscientist scholar. It's surprising how much these scientists know about the humanities. I recall Robert Oppenheimer, testifying before a congressional committee, telling how as a boy he loved walking through the library stacks in his town, and checking out and soaking up the classics he found there. I doubt whether many scholars in the humanities could say, 'In my youth I soaked up science.'

"Still, as a group, I suspect that scientists, and engineers, tend to be more one-track-minded than humanists, and this is a serious problem."

Why?

"Because scientists are becoming more influential and powerful in their effect on human life through experiments in new fields such as recombinant DNA research. New scientific discoveries in communications, and robotics, can profoundly affect the way people live, and work, and behave; how the human race will evolve. No one wants such power in the hands of men and women insensitive to the human dimension of what they're doing."

While scientists, given their new importance, need an awareness of the world outside their specialties, he called it comparably important for nonscientists to gain a better grasp of science: for sociologists to know some biochemistry, and political scientists some plasma physics.

"The time is ripe for the second coming of C. P. Snow, for the emergence of a writer-philosopher who can carry Snow's 'two-cultures' thesis into an era in which the tremendous increase in the flow of information, largely as a result of more sophisticated computers, threatens to unhinge mankind. Information, because of its sheer bulk, is becoming another form of life-threatening pollution. Experiments have shown that mice crowded into too small a space will go berserk. I'm afraid too much information impacting on human beings can have the same effect unless they can be taught to live with it; to avoid retreating deeper and deeper into their own narrow fields.

"What makes Princeton significant in the battle against narrowness is not that individuals in other universities don't recognize the problem and try to confront it. They do. When I was a boy, my uncle, a professor of chemical engineering in a large Midwestern university, belonged to a 'dinner club,' a group of professors of various kindred disciplines who met monthly for a good meal and to talk about what they were doing. This sort of thing went on in other disciplines and other universities, and still does.

"The difference is that at Princeton it's institutionalized, facilitated by the teaching and administering arrangements I've described. Princeton is the essense of interaction. It symbolizes a virtue that larger institutions respect but by their size and nature are discouraged or prevented from practicing."

21

"Even those students locked into career studies... seem less 'preprofessional' here..., more disposed to broaden themselves while they have the chance."

ELAINE SHOWALTER

Despite its historic halls and traditions, Princeton, said Elaine Showalter, "because it is undergraduate-centered, is pervaded by a spirit of youthfulness unusual in research universities." This spirit greatly appealed to her during her nine years as a Princeton "faculty wife" teaching at another university, and still appeals to her now that she is a tenured Princeton professor.

"Collaborative" she called the attitude of most Princeton professors toward students. "There is a mutual exchange between the two which I find most rewarding. I hope I contribute to my students' maturing intellectually; I know they help keep me *im*mature—in a good way, taking 'maturity' to mean to some extent rigidity, narrowness, and conformity. I find I get new ideas from students, new interests. Some of their openness and curiosity rubs off on me. I don't want to be in a place where I relate only to senior scholars working in my field, at my level. I love knowing that every year the

---

A prolific writer, especially on Victorian literature and women writers, Showalter—B.A. Bryn Mawr and M.A. Brandeis—earned her Ph.D. and taught at the University of California at Davis, then at Douglass College, University of Delaware, and Rutgers (Distinguished Professor of English). Elected to the Academy of Literary Studies in 1981, she has served on the Supervising Committee of the English Institute and the editorial board of Publications of the Modern Language Association. Her books include *A Literature of Their Own: British Women Novelists from Brontë to Lessing*, and (as editor) *The New Feminist Criticism*.

freshmen will be eighteen!—and I'll be working with some of them."

Princeton's spirit of youthfulness manifests itself in many ways, she said. For example, "I was surprised and impressed, when I was being considered for an appointment here, by how friendly and informal people were. I felt genuine enthusiasm for the 'sample' lecture I gave. It's the usual academic style for people to seem somewhat jaded on such occasions, to have a 'seen-it-all-before' attitude; *hauteur;* distance. Here people seemed willing to be excited and to let it show.

"Later in the hiring process I was talking with Dean Lemonick in his Nassau Hall office one Saturday morning when President Bowen dropped in, joined the conversation, suddenly said, 'Shall I make you some coffee?' I was startled but said, 'Yes, I'd like that.' He took off for his own office and coffee machine, was back in a few minutes with my cup. To this day I can't help laughing when I try to imagine this happening at the other Ivy League university whose offer I was weighing at the time."

As a specialist in gender matters, has she found the gap between male and female Princeton students to be unusually narrow, owing to the atmosphere she had been describing?

She stopped eating her lunch and looked out over the snow-covered Prospect gardens.

"Maybe—but not a lot. I *was* surprised by the interest of male students in the feminist work I've done. I'd anticipated some hostility, found none. In fact, the contrary: Half the students in my Gender and Literary Theory course are men. From my teaching elsewhere, and from talking with colleagues, I'd conclude the situation is rather unusual here, but the fact is, the college years in any coed institution are apt to be the most egalitarian of most people's lives; the time when men and women, however much they've been separated and unequally treated before, and may be after, do so many things together. This student period is a culture of its own, at both the undergraduate and graduate levels. Intellectually and socially, there is an unusual amount of equality, many things done together or in parallel—academic projects, sports, career counseling.

"As the percentage of tenured women on university faculties increases, this atmosphere will be enhanced—and Princeton has made a better start than most toward eventual balance, has brought in women scholars at an unusually high rate."

She gives the "spirit of youthfulness and openness" some credit for Princeton's having an outstanding women's studies program, "one of the strongest among Ivy League schools and by far the strongest among those only recently coeducational. There has been pressure from students everywhere—encouraged, of course, by a lot of publicity over the past decades about the women's movement—to develop such programs; but Princeton has gone about it in an unusual and I think characteristic way. Elsewhere they've said, 'Let's get someone in to "cover" women's studies.' Princeton's approach has been, 'This is one of those rare phenomena, a new field of intellectual inquiry. Let's build our program the way you build one in molecular biology: a research team of people who will stimulate each other.'

"At the same time the English department hired me, they also hired Sandra Gilbert, one of the leading feminist critics in the world. We were good friends, had worked together, but never in the close and mutually reinforcing way we can now. Both of us had been approached by other universities wanting to hire one or the other. Princeton wanted us both!

"It's amazing the way ideas develop when you get the right people together—and this was the first university to take this revolutionary approach to women's studies."

She credits Princeton's youthful flexibility but also good communication between faculty and administration. "It's easier to coordinate when you don't have an enormous bureaucratic structure, with some people doing one thing, some another, and some spinning off into space: and of course, this is not a mega-university where the ability to discuss things one-on-one is lost."

She paused as the student waiter started to clear the table. Would she explain for the reader—not to mention the writer—exactly what is meant by "women's studies."

"Women's studies deals with the achievements and roles of women, and with theories of gender, across the disciplines. Since for centuries all knowledge has been in effect men's studies—history, for example, being all men's wars and men's politics and men's trading—now we must study what women were doing all that time, as writers, members of the labor force, and so on, in order to understand what was really going on.

"Eventually all disciplines will deal with the expressions and achievements of men *and* women; but meanwhile research on women and gender theory have become important areas of disciplinary specialization which will continue to grow."

Did anything surprise her about Princeton when she joined the faculty?

"Yes: How hard we work!" Harder than faculties elsewhere? "I think so. Not only is there the commitment to students, on which Princeton puts such a high priority—the personal advising and conferring in addition to lecturing and precepting—but all faculty, especially senior professors, are responsibly involved in some aspect of administration. All this plus their own research, and the outside commitments a senior scholar has." In her case, the latter are numerous. As a leading authority on Victorian and American literature and on women's writing, she is much in demand for lectures, serves on many national committees and editorial boards, and is drawn into controversies—most recently in the *New York Times Book Review*—over such questions as whether "women writers" should be singled out as such or dealt with simply as "writers." Her view, enormously oversimplified: both.

" 'Hard' is probably the wrong word for how one works here. It's time- and energy-demanding, working with students, but it's fun, too. And the committee work isn't 'hard' if that implies drudgery. You get to know your colleagues, learn what's going on in your own and other professions."

I quoted something Professor Robert L. Geddes, longtime dean of the architecture school, had said to me: "The most important students in a university are the faculty. If they're not learning, and growing, nobody is." She nodded emphatic agreement.

As a fellow of Stevenson Hall during the 1960s, she had come to know many students—graduate and undergraduate—but she had still been surprised by their "creative diversity" when she joined the faculty.

No, she did not mean diversity *among* students, said by Carl Schorske and others to be greater at larger public universities, but diversity *within* individual students. "The navy ROTC student taking ceramics and making lovely pots; the physicist in creative writing; the English major who plans to dance professionally when she graduates. Even those locked into career studies— medicine, law, engineering—seem less 'preprofessional' here than at other places I know of, more disposed to broaden themselves while they have the chance."

She thought that contributed significantly to the atmosphere of youthfulness at Princeton.

"If athletes here learn to respect one another regardless of race, so do students who sweat out the senior thesis together."

22

CONRAD D. SNOWDEN

Some twenty years ago, Princeton and other all-white or nearly all-white universities began not only to admit but to recruit significant numbers of black students. How each has been affected by its black students is a subject for scholarly research.

My aim in talking with Conrad Snowden was more modest: to get his insight into the kind of place Princeton is for black students, in comparison with other Ivy League and similar universities.

He seemed the person to ask, given his thirteen years of personal and official contact with black Princeton students, first as director of the Third World Center, later as chairman of the university's Minority Affairs Committee, and most recently as chairman of a sub-committee on race relations that spent three months digging into that subject in conversations with individuals and groups on campus.

Understandably to anyone who has dealt with the sensitive question of race relations in predominantly white universities, Snowden drew back from my question. He said that although he has been immersed in Princeton affairs, he has not studied race relations on other campuses and could not make an informed com-

---

A graduate of Howard University, where he taught and administered after doing graduate work at the University of Chicago, Snowden taught at Simmons College in Boston before coming to Princeton in 1970 as assistant dean of the faculty and the Graduate School, and lecturer in sociology and philosophy. He later became associate provost. He has been a special consultant to the U.S. Office of Education.

parison; moreover, "black students, anywhere, are not a monolithic body for whom any one person can speak"; and finally, he was reluctant to generalize "because if there is one thing I've learned, it is that race relations among college students today are complicated far beyond most people's ability to imagine, and the last thing I want to do is oversimplify them."

What about taking a few of the characteristics of Princeton that are generally acknowledged to be distinctive, and assessing their meaning to black students?

Yes, he would attempt that, with the understanding that "anything I say about black students in general may well prove to be wrong for an individual black student."

In our several conversations, over the next few weeks, he divided the Princeton characteristics into three categories: academic, administrative, and "atmospheric." And he emphasized how black students' perceptions of Princeton's "advantages" do not always coincide with those of white students.

"Because of the academic arrangements that guarantee Princeton undergraduates more direct individual attention from faculty members than is available elsewhere, undergraduates can't as easily 'get lost' at Princeton as they can at larger, less intimate places. This is seen as a major advantage by most students, and you might expect it to be especially appreciated by blacks coming into a strange, predominantly white world. But the truth is, a student likes being thrust into a close relationship with his professors only to the degree that he or she is comfortable with them. For most white students this is no problem, most professors being white; nor is it for some blacks.

"But all blacks don't arrive at Princeton feeling comfortable with whites, much less white professors. Society has made many black students hesitant and even suspicious. It has given them negative expectations as often as positive, and the result is that some don't necessarily want to be close to their professors—not at first; and in some cases, never. To 'get lost,' in the sense of being allowed to keep their distance, is exactly what many black students want, or think they want, at least to the extent of being inconspicuous.

"This was true of a number of women students, too, when they first came to Princeton, and were not as numerous as now. I'm told they, too, wanted to feel inconspicuous, not because they felt inferior or were afraid of embarrassing themselves, but because they had not had, personally or as a group, the experience of being in this kind of place. They were concerned, not without historical reason, that they might be seen by their male peers as not worthy to be here. If inconspicuous, they were less likely to invite judgment."

In his official and unofficial listening to black students recently, Snowden had been "surprised at the depth of concern of bright black kids that they are considered less deserving of being here than they feel themselves to be. They feel they belong, many having come with good records from good schools. They don't expect to be treated as better or worse than white students, but as equally good. And many were unhappy that white students seemed to underrate them simply because of race.

"Generally speaking," he said, "all students, black and white, come here feeling intimidated. Even those who have been great successes in high school feel, 'Everybody here is smarter than I am, and there's no hope for me.' But white students don't usually come scared *and* suspicious, thinking, 'This place is not only difficult, it may even be against me.' And on some level of consciousness, many blacks do have that suspicion. Society instills it in them. I suspect they would feel the same entering any other Ivy League college, but the feeling can be very intense here, and more unremitting, partly because it *is* harder here to 'get lost.'

"For black students who can come to terms with its 'closeness,' and increasing numbers seem to be doing so, Princeton offers things they can't as easily get elsewhere: for one, the greater chance of being taught by, and getting personally acquainted with, leading scholars. This varies from department to department, but students do encounter a faculty unusually devoted to undergraduate teaching. Because the students expect individual attention from their professors, and because they expect at least decent teaching, Princeton students are more likely to complain if they encounter what they consider poor teaching, and to have their complaints heeded—just as professors, recognizing the strength of this long-standing tradition, are less likely to be remiss in fulfilling their teaching responsibilities."

Turning to *administrative* characteristics, Snowden singled out two as distinguishing Princeton and having special meaning for black students. "First, partly because of its size and partly because of tradition, this university thinks of and deals with students as individuals and not as groups or blocs. Larger universities tend to deal with students in blocs, allowing a part of the group to speak for the whole. We don't. The place is too small and the concentration on undergraduates is too intense; too many strands can be seen running through every rope. You couldn't tune out individual voices here even if you wanted to. One hears too much of what is going on not to know pretty much which students are dissatisfied, and why, and whose fault it is, or whose fault they think it is.

"Second, the strongly established feeling among administrators here is that serious problems, including race relations, should be confronted and solved in a collaborative way. There is a high degree of confidence that if you bring people together and talk candidly about your differences and complaints and problems, the *process* will probably help even if the problems are not actually resolved.

"This feeling exists among students, as well. And students have been woven into the operational fabric of this place to a degree very unusual in research universities. The Undergraduate Student Government (USG) is unusually active, and students sit on a wide variety of important university committees. So, the opportunities are exceptional here for student views to get a hearing, periodically or when some issue is nearing crisis and needs some talking and thinking out.

"For example, a Forum for Interracial Communication was set up several years ago by black and white students, in collaboration with the USG. It held open meetings, some attended by more than a hundred students, others smaller. This went on for two years. It took up such questions as what the eating clubs could do to encourage more participation by black students, and what the Third World Center could do to bring in more whites. That structure was revived a couple of years later.

"More recently, when the *Daily Princetonian* focused attention on several problems in campus race relations, President Bowen asked me, as chairman of the Minority Affairs Committee, to form a special subcommittee to provide a more comprehensive picture of race relations on campus and to identify concrete ways specific problems might be ameliorated. That group was made up of four administrators and five students.

"We held open meetings over a period of three months with a dozen campus groups and many individuals, and one result was the forming by the USG of a permanent committee on race relations to continue the dialogue on student-to-student relations, and social life.

"The positive aspects, for all students, of Princeton's administrative characteristics are obvious. But for some black students there are negative aspects, too.

"First, for black students who are ideologically and politically oriented, Princeton's way of dealing with individuals rather than groups can be unattractive because these students may want to represent, and speak with authority for, their group. The relatively easy access of individual students to top administrators tends to make it difficult for the would-be ideological leaders to be very effective.

"Second, Princeton's reliance on the consultative process means it sometimes takes this university longer to solve a problem than some students think it should, or than it seems to take elsewhere. In part, of course, this is because Princeton sees microcosms of diversity. The more eyes you have to do the looking, the more diversity you're going to see; the more complexity. You are less likely, then, to arrive at quick and simple solutions. Those you do arrive at are more likely to be practical and durable, and less likely to create unfairness to other groups while solving the problems of one. But students don't always have the patience to appreciate these points. So Princeton has a reputation for being rather slow to respond to social pressures. However, it also has a reputation for moving ahead more vigorously once it does respond, and with better planning—and better results—than many places. Still, students feeling grievances are sometimes troubled by Princeton's deliberateness.

"Princeton very rarely makes too-quick decisions just to 'get students off our backs.' As a result, some students feel we're putting them off, that we don't value their views. But I have seen the anguish this university goes through to make sure it's doing the right thing; have seen us hold up a decision until we've had the views of students as well as faculty; and then, after more reflection, change our minds. Some students find it frustrating that we can't be pressured into making large political gestures but have to be persuaded by reason. Actually, students are effective here in ways some don't recognize; but this doesn't prevent their fearing cooptation or feeling unhappy with the Princeton administrative style."

Under "atmosphere," Snowden included the sense of the past evoked by Princeton's campus; also its non-urban location and its small size. "All of these tend to affect blacks differently from whites.

"To many whites, just the look of the campus recalls historical associations and achievements to be proud of. I don't want to make too much of this, but insofar as blacks have only fairly recently and tentatively been accepted as full-fledged Americans, black students are bound to feel some ambivalence toward American history. And it's harder to escape it here.

"To white students, Woodrow Wilson is a kind of hero, and today's blacks can be grateful to him for some educational innovations that now benefit them; as political realists they can understand why he discouraged black students from coming here, and took so little interest in the plight of black Americans during his U.S. presidency; but forgetting is much harder.

"I see nothing inherent in today's Princeton to discourage black students from coming here, but it's difficult for some who come from places where prejudice still exists, to a place where they can still feel a history of prejudice. It requires a real exercise of will on the part of some blacks to select Princeton with its historic associations with the white aristocracy, and its past reputation as a very hard place for black students to enter.

"Most people, whites and blacks, find it hard to believe that an institution as rooted in tradition as Princeton is can have changed as much as Princeton has over the last twenty years. But black students discover, in time, that this is so; and we know, as we watch blacks come back for reunions and participate in the Association of Black Princeton Alumni, that many end up with much the same 'family feeling' for the place that white alumni have, though less easily come by.

"All in all, there are tremendous advantages to the Princeton experience for blacks, but purchased at the price of some discomfort. Precisely because of the environment, there may be a special satisfaction for blacks in 'making it' here."

Can it be made more comfortable for them? Is Snowden optimistic or pessimistic about the future of race relations at Princeton?

"I'm an optimist by nature. I believe any problem that can be identified can be solved, given an institution as determined to improve things as I believe Princeton is.

"As I told you—and my experience as chairman of the race relations subcommittee made me feel this more strongly—I am suspicious of easy solutions, and of people who glibly advance them. Some naïveté and overenthusiasm are excusable in people of good will, but glibness is something else. Those who make less of a serious problem by proposing simplistic solutions can really cause trouble."

Can he suggest a real, if complicated, solution?

"I believe when people of one race can honestly say to those of another, 'I want to understand you, or as much about you as I can about any friend,' that will take us a long way. And I was pleased to discover how many students, black and white, seemed ready to do this. But I was depressed to discover how many black students have the idea that white students simply don't like them. Out of these attitudes—on both sides—tensions come; and more dialogue is the only way to reach the truth, which surely is that most white students and black students at a place like Princeton don't dislike each other; they don't *know* each other. They're often simply strangers!

"Hearing some blacks talk—in our race relations meetings—about how painful relations between the races have been for them, I was personally affected. I found that if I shifted my attitude only a tiny bit, I could become as suspicious of whites as some of the students were. Walking on Nassau Street, when something a little out of the ordinary happened to me, I could think, 'Was that racism?' And that's a question I hadn't asked for years. I began to look at my own good white friends a little differently. It was a tremendous emotional experience. I saw myself in a different way. *I was vulnerable, too, and what the students were saying I found painfully believable.*"

But over all he was encouraged by what came out of the subcommittee sessions. "At one meeting a white student said, 'This is the first time I've been at a meeting where black kids were every bit our equals.' I ended up believing that when you give young people enough time, in the right setting, to follow their instincts, they move toward the light."

If an optimist, Snowden is not a romantic one. "If we could solve the race problem at Princeton, there would remain the social-class problem: how can you influence lower-income black students to respect upper-income blacks, and vice versa? Actually, even today, there are at least as many economic and class tensions at Princeton as racial ones; as many political as personal.

"The great equalizer," he concluded, "is the Princeton academic program. Superficially, racial and other tensions are probably increased by the fact that students have to work so hard here; they don't have as much time and energy to devote to bridging racial and other gaps as they might have elsewhere. But on a deeper level, the work brings them together. Old prejudices seem pretty pointless to students who are locked together in an enterprise as demanding and dignified as serious learning. If athletes here learn to respect one another regardless of race, so do students who sweat out the senior thesis together. What we all need, to erase racial barriers, is something important in common: a love, a fear. And making it at Princeton academically involves both of those. I guess that's the real source of my optimism."

"The most important thing for educators to be thinking about, from grade school to graduate school, is how students can be turned on by being encouraged to make subjects their own."

23

DONALD E. STOKES

"There is only one secret of education," said Donald Stokes, "and considering there's only one, it's remarkable how well kept it is." The secret? "The best way to learn something is to teach it to yourself—and that comes very close to stating the core of Princeton's educational philosophy and what distinguishes it from most universities.

"It may be paradoxical that Princeton, while committed to encouraging students to teach themselves, has a faculty so committed to teaching them. But teaching students to teach themselves is far more difficult than any other approach."

Would he draw on Princeton's Woodrow Wilson School of Public and International Affairs, of which he is dean, for an illustration of how students are taught to teach themselves?

Yes, he would like to do that, because he believes the Wilson school, in its values and teaching methods, is

---

Donald E. Stokes—A.B. Princeton (1951), Ph.D. Yale—is dean of Princeton's Woodrow Wilson School of Public and International Affairs. He has taught at Yale, Oxford, the Australian National University, the University of the West Indies, and the University of Michigan, where he was chairman of the political science department and dean of the graduate school. He is coauthor of *The American Voter, Elections and the Political Order,* and *Political Change in Britain.*

"Princeton in microcosm." And without hesitation he cited "the undergraduate policy conference" as a teaching device that illustrates both the school's and the university's philosophy.

A policy conference, he said, is a group of fifteen or so juniors—helped by three to five seniors and supervised by a faculty member—collaborating in the exploration of a complex current public issue, domestic or foreign, and arriving at a set of practical recommendations as to how the responsible government or government agency should deal with it. (Juniors are first-year students in the school, admitted at the end of sophomore year in sufficient numbers to make up four conferences each fall term. For both juniors and seniors the conference counts as one course.)

"The conference idea was born in 1930 with the school itself, whose founders believed the way to prepare students to deal in later life with thorny public issues was to have them do so as students, in a rigorous academic way but under real-life conditions; on their own for much of the time, but with expert help and criticism at every stage. They thought this would help bridge the gap between the abstractions of their social science studies and the concreteness of life."

He offered a step-by-step description of a process that "has changed some over the years but remains faithful to the original concept; that originated separately from preceptorials but is extremely compatible with them."

Step 1. "The school, every fall, chooses four conference topics; that is, four public issues worthy of a term's hard work. The first year—'Philippine Independence,' 'The Polish Corridor,' 'Unemployment Insurance,' and 'Muscle Shoals,' the precursor to TVA. In 1985-86 they were 'A Changing Society and the Nation's Children,' 'The Future Uses of Space,' 'U.S. Policy Toward Southern Africa,' and 'U.S.-Latin American Relations.'"

2. "A faculty member—or sometimes a distinguished outside expert—is chosen to lead each conference, serving as 'counsellor and adviser.' Each junior is assigned to one of these issue-centered groups, with some concern for the student's own academic interests.

"The faculty or outside leaders are people who, like the Princeton faculty generally, get their kicks not from parading their wisdom but from watching students grow; who want to pass the baton to them, not let them be passive."

3. "Each group is briefed on the issue by the faculty leader and visiting experts who have included a former president of the U.S., cabinet members, U.S. senators, heads of government agencies and even of foreign governments. The issue is thoroughly discussed at this point and may be researched by the group in a field setting, with an entire conference going to Washington or even abroad."

4. "The leader and the group divide the conference topic into component aspects, and each junior is assigned to research intensively and write a paper on one aspect. This is a solo effort, but is expected to contribute measurably to the group's final product. This paper may go through several revisions as a result of rigorous criticism from the leader and advice from the seniors, who have been through this themselves and are called 'commissioners' because in the early days each conference was set up along the lines of a federal investigative commission."

5. "Every junior—and senior—in a group studies the final draft of every other junior's paper, and then, in a meeting of that conference chaired by a senior and observed by the leader, the juniors make oral presentations of what they have learned *and decided* about the topic. That is, they not only have to get the facts, isolate the relevant ones, and write about them concisely, they

have to get up in a 'public meeting' and speak for their findings, pointedly and persuasively, and defend them in a question period that may go on far into the night. And of course the juniors as a group serve as an informed and critical audience for each member's presentation."

6. "The seniors in each group, having studied the juniors' papers and heard them presented and defended orally, draft a set of recommendations for dealing with the issue that will pool the juniors' insights and embody their strongest points. This draft is studied and debated by the students, under the leader's critical eye, until there is general agreement as to what should go into the final paper.

"Agreement is not always unanimous. Students may, and occasionally do, submit dissents. We don't encourage that, because we want them to learn to negotiate creatively, to make concessions—even compromises—without sacrificing important principles; that is, to produce real solutions, not just win votes; to be stubborn in defense of their beliefs but not so stubborn they deal themselves out of the process.

"These final papers are written as if they were going to the government or agency dealing with the issue, and often do go to them. Many agencies know about our policy conference and welcome a look at our product, particularly when one of their members has participated in our early discussions."

7. "Finally, after the joint paper has been closed, an outside expert who has read it comes in and critiques it for the group, and lets them respond. This is a key part of the conference. I often hear these visitors express awe and wonder at how deeply the students have informed themselves, how close they have come to the hard realities, how far away they are from simply striking ideological poses, from believing complex issues—es-

pecially those involving science and technology—can be disposed of by an exercise in ideology."

Summing up, Stokes said, "Some conferences are better than others, some students benefit more than others; but it's impossible to listen to alumni without concluding the power of the conference is astonishing." He said George Shultz '42 once told him that as a U.S. marine in the Far East during World War II he, thanks to a conference on American foreign policy, "was about the only man in my outfit who had any idea what might have caused the war."

He said most students come out of the conference with more respect for the social sciences, having found how history, politics, psychology, sociology can contribute to the solving of a hard practical problem. "They learn how it feels to become so deeply immersed in a problem that you feel you 'own it.' They learn how large, complex, often dirty problems can be divided into manageable pieces, the pieces studied separately, and the whole thing put together again. They develop a capacity for looking across great gulfs and seeing there is another side to most issues; that few things are as simple as they look; that problems have their own structures.

"This is teaching the hard way, but students learn something about learning they're not likely to forget."

Do other public affairs schools have programs like the conference? "No. Our peer schools at other universities typically have nothing to do with undergraduates. We now have a renowned graduate program, but we started out as an undergraduate school and remain very much concerned with undergraduates."

Could the principles back of the conference be adopted by teachers in secondary schools?

"To some extent. It's depressing how much that's wrong with American education at all levels is that it's

essentially a passive experience. Many Princeton methods, including the conference, are too costly for less
well-endowed colleges and universities, let alone high
schools. But budget limits are too often used to justify
poor teaching. However tight their budgets, the most
important thing for educators to be thinking about,
from grade school to graduate school, is how students
can be turned on by being encouraged to make subjects
their own."

"At Princeton nearly all disciplines are taught as if they were creative arts." 24

THEODORE R. WEISS

"Woodrow Wilson would have been amazed— and alarmed!—if he had been told at the turn of the century that his educational philosophy would one day make this university uncommonly hospitable to creative arts courses. But," said poet Theodore Weiss, who for twenty years has taught poetry in Princeton's creative writing program, "that is exactly what has happened.

"Wilson believed that thinking, feeling human beings cannot be mass-produced by a university, so he fostered small-group teaching, attention to the individual student, independent work, close ties between faculty and students—all of which are essential to creative arts instruction. The kind of teaching Wilson institutionalized at Princeton is the kind you have to have in the arts.

"At the same time, Princeton's curricular conservatism, also fostered by Wilson, meant that creative arts courses had a harder time getting established here than at most universities. But when they did come— starting with creative writing in the 1930s, but not expanding much, and not gathering much steam, till

Having taught at Yale, the Universities of North Carolina and Maryland, and Bard College, Weiss—A.B. Muhlenberg, M.A. Columbia— came to Princeton in 1966 as poet-in-residence and joined the faculty two years later. With his wife, Renée, he publishes *The Quarterly Review of Literature* from an on-campus office. His poems have appeared in most literary magazines, many anthologies, and eleven all-Weiss collections, the most recent in 1985: *A Living Room.*

134

the 1960s—they could take their size and shape from regular courses and their color from the institution, because at Princeton nearly all disciplines are taught as if they were creative arts."

How has this affected arts instruction at Princeton?

"Students here are accustomed to working together in a hard-headed workshop atmosphere that encourages intimacy and awareness among them, so when they enter arts courses they're ready to participate actively, draw each other out, achieve a kind of *ensemble* playing in which they learn as much from each other as from the teacher. And the teacher, if I'm an example, learns most of all. I wouldn't have gone on teaching if it hadn't been that way.

"Any kind of creative work involves self-revelation, so in the informality of the workshop, students mobilize their individual strengths, relate to each other, become good friends—not superficially, as in, say, a club relationship, but in important, deep internal ways.

"It's hazardous to generalize, to compare Princeton with other universities, but I believe the intimacy among students here is uncommon, and certainly that between faculty and students is. On the train coming away from a visit to another Ivy League school I sat behind two undergraduates and overheard one say, 'I'm hiding out from that professor. He's not going to see or hear from me all term.' That sort of thing would be hard to pull off at Princeton."

Weiss paused and threw up his hands in mock amazement at finding himself "applauding a Princeton I have so often cried out against" for its academic conservatism which has led, in his opinion, to an under-appreciation of the arts. "I can still get in an argument with some fellow members of the English department faculty"—he has taught Shakespeare to undergraduates and modern poetry to graduate students— "over whether writing courses are a slightly frivolous enterprise, entertaining, but for leisure time. It's interesting that in education's early days the scholars were the curators, the preservers. It took the scientists to give the arts academic respectability, to establish that *doing something new* was a legitimate aspect of education."

So convinced is Weiss of the importance of arts courses to orthodox learning that he would require all English majors to take at least one course in creative writing.

"In the normal English course, students deal with finished pieces of literary work. In a creative writing course they study works in progress—their own, their fellow students', sometimes the instructor's—at different stages. It's the difference between moving from the outside in—from the finished work to some comprehension of how it was done—and moving from the inside out, shaping something of your own so that others can take it in and get from it what you mean them to.

"There is more compatibility between the two approaches than is generally realized. Reading classics helps a student develop taste, an ability to look critically at a piece of work, including his own. Making something of his own gives him an intensity of focus he can then bring to the study of literature—and of himself and his own inner life. We tend to get the livelier students in the arts courses, and help to sharpen their perceptiveness for their other courses. There's something subduing about lectures, necessary as they are. In creative workshops, as in preceptorials, you plunge in and argue rather than sit back and be entertained."

Weiss said the student activism and generally yeasty tone of the 1960s was good for Princeton in that it "created pressures that led to making the curriculum more supple, more open to the arts and to innovation generally. The number of arts students, faculty, and courses has rapidly increased. Creative writing, visual arts, theater and dance are nearly, but not quite, accepted as 'majors' now; meanwhile a student can do a creative thesis for an established department with a member of the creative arts faculty as one of two thesis advisers."

But, he said, Princeton's conservatism remains a problem in a different way. "Princeton still has more required courses for undergraduates than most comparable universities, and this means a student has to fight harder to find the time and justification for arts courses, even though credits are now given for them on a pass/fail basis."

Is Princeton a bad place, then, for the would-be artist?

"No, it's a good place. Serious artists need the best possible education to prepare them to deal with their own material. They have more to fear than most students from narrowness, from a too early concentration on their own specialty. But of course most students who study creative arts here don't mean to make careers of them. They take them precisely to broaden themselves, to have a once-in-a-lifetime experience of being a practicing artist before going into medicine, law, business, and so on."

Another attribute of Princeton relevant to its ability to educate students in the arts is the campus, "a work of art in itself, an illustration of what man and nature can do, working together. The planning and planting have to affect artists; poets, certainly, even though poets don't write much about nature nowadays. To live here is so rare an experience that smugness can be a problem." But he does miss the bookshops and coffee shops of larger university towns.

Is it easier to teach and write poetry in a place like Princeton than in a city-based university?

"Yes, I'd say for most of us it invites the muse more than a chaotic or ugly place would. T. S. Eliot had to leave his bank teller's job in London and go to Switzerland to concentrate on finishing *The Wasteland*—suggesting that to write well even about chaos you need a little peace and quiet!"

He said he greatly envies his students "their chance to submerge themselves for four years, withdraw from the turbulence of life to study parts of it. This place has the characteristics and advantages of an artists' colony. It's a luxury, but a useful, usable, even a necessary one; a chance to collect oneself, to live among kindred spirits, before plunging back into the turbulence.

"Princeton expects great things of its students and graduates, or why is all this invested in them? Even the senior thesis is a work of art! In a day when we are being overrun by mass production, it gives each student a chance to concentrate like an artist on one piece of work, under the eye of a professor who treats each student as an individual worth spending time on. Our students don't know how lucky they are! Or maybe they do."

"Human beings everywhere need to discover, and recognize, and act out of their similarities, their connectedness as human beings, their interrelatedness, if they expect to survive."

25

THEODORE ZIOLKOWSKI

His work as a scholar in recent years had centered on German romanticism of the late eighteenth and early nineteenth centuries, said Theodore Ziolkowski, "a movement which gave many modern institutions their present shapes. In fact, the book I'm now working on deals with four such institutions: mines, museums, madhouses, and universities."

To his surprise, "the more deeply I studied the University of Berlin, which was founded by romantic thinkers in 1810—the first university that can be called 'modern'—the more clearly I could perceive Princeton and appreciate the characteristic that most distinguishes it from other universities.

"The German romantics saw all being and all reality as a unity, and this concept of 'wholeness' was reflected in their university. In line with romantic thinking, they regarded all disciplines as parts of a great interrelated whole, saw not the separateness of different philoso-

A much-published scholar in the field of German and comparative literature, Ziolkowski is a graduate of Duke University, studied at the University of Innsbruck in Austria, earned his Ph.D. at Yale, and taught there and at Columbia before coming to Princeton in 1964. He became chairman of the Department of Germanic Languages and Literatures and then was appointed dean of the Graduate School in 1979. Three of his published books have been on Hermann Hesse. His *Fictional Transfigurations of Jesus* won the James Russell Lowell Prize for criticism.

phies but their connectedness, saw languages as related families rather than as discrete structures. They anticipated Darwinism, which emerged from their view of biology as a connected whole. And so on through the disciplines.

"All this at a time when the French universities as reorganized by Napoleon were mainly professional training schools; the English universities were really undergraduate colleges preparing young gentlemen to enter Parliament; and German universities tended to be dueling societies. Radically for their time, the romantics saw the proper business of a university as the *pursuit of knowledge,* including the discovering of new knowledge; and out of this attitude came the modern notion of academic freedom: freedom to seek truth wherever the search might lead.

"The more I studied that university, the more clearly I saw Princeton as surely the world's closest approximation to it today, to its ideals of what a university ought to be: not only because of Princeton's smallness—which is not a virtue in and of itself and actually has some disadvantages—but because it has kept alive the spirit of wholeness better than any other university I know of in the world.

"This is manifested in many ways, at many levels: in the unity here between learner and teacher, working together, giving to and taking from each other and forming a smooth continuum from the lowliest freshman to the most distinguished scholar; in the unity between faculty and administration, a unity not possible in large, complex institutions where departments compete as self-centered adversaries and regard the administration as almost an outsider, an unloved umpire. It is in the unity among disciplines that flow together partly because they are joined in an unusually large number of interdisciplinary programs, but mainly because of close professional and personal relationships among professors representing them.

"As an example of the latter, some of my Princeton colleagues from whom I, as a professor of comparative literature, have learned the most are in fields such as engineering, physics, biology—fields that would be the most remote from me in a larger, less unified place. I spoke last week at the University of Toronto on 'Existential Anxieties of Engineers,' drawing on literary examples all the way from Faust—did you know, in addition to being a magician and alchemist he was an engineer, a builder of dikes and canals?—to figures in contemporary novels. This subject fascinates me! The engineer, in literature and in life, is a particularly apt symbol of man in a technological society, torn between what he is rationally and scientifically capable of doing or building, and what irrationally he feels he ought, or ought not, to do or build. The point is, I never would have tackled this subject if I had not been thrown in with engineers on a day-to-day basis at Princeton, and if as a consequence engineers were not among my closest friends.

"Princeton's wholeness is exemplified—and I regard exemplification as extremely important—by its physical appearance; not only by the relative compactness of its campus but by the design of it. From a certain spot on campus one can see the library, which might be called the mind of the place; the chapel, which might be called its soul; and, craning the neck a bit, Nassau Hall, with its administrative offices and Faculty Room, which might be called its heart. By moving a few steps one can see buildings devoted to sciences, and to all of the humanities.

"The dominating force here, as it was at the University of Berlin, is centripetal, drawing all toward the center. This is true even of the professional schools—of engineering, of architecture, of public and international affairs. Elsewhere, faculty and students of such schools are drawn to their own centers and away from the universities. Their force is centrifugal."

He finds unity in the relationship between the
Graduate School and the undergraduate college. "It's in
the way our graduate and undergraduate students inter-
mix. Not only do both attend classes on the same
campus but often they attend the same classes. Last year
some 250 undergraduates, most but not all of them
seniors, took graduate-level courses, while some 430
graduate students took undergraduate-level courses. I
don't think any other research university has the same
degree of cross-fertilization. And of course both are
taught by the same faculty, which emphasizes the similarities between the two types of students, whereas at
most universities it is their differentness that gets
emphasized by the use of different faculties for each."

He said the intermixing of graduate and undergraduate students at Princeton "is more academic than social,
but they do meet outside the classroom and laboratory—on the tennis courts, at the gym, and in intra-
mural sports. The production of an opera every year
involves mainly undergraduates, but also some graduate
students.

"The main university library is used by both, and it's a
hub of activity to an extent not true at other places
where libraries are great but less accessible and where
there are separate ones for undergraduates.

"Princeton also is unusual if not unique in providing
housing for most graduate students: about two thirds
last year, single ones at the Graduate College, and the
married in university apartments, both very near the
main campus, which contributes to the sense of unity
here.

"And the Graduate School dean is closer to the
central university administration here than at most
similar places; more intimately involved in the whole
educational process. At many universities, the graduate
dean is little more than a glorified registrar who counts
students and takes care of the budget but is not involved

with the departments, which set their own standards and 'let the dean know.' At one university with a first-rate graduate school, the German department is almost completely independent. My opposite number at another place told me he hadn't been in his president's office in two years. Here, I sit on the president's cabinet, which meets once a week at lunch, and I run into him in Nassau Hall where we both have offices."

A parting question: Granted Princeton "approximates the ideals" of the University of Berlin, is this *good?*—to resemble an institution that flourished more than a century ago?

"Yes. The principle of wholeness seems to me very timely today."

Why?

"Reality thrusts itself on us today in bits and pieces; fragmented. It used to be that social forces helped to keep individuals whole: the family, the neighborhood, the community, the church, all exerted a unifying pressure. But for many people these institutions no longer have that effect. The family is so often broken by divorce or strained by generational and other misunderstandings; people move in and out of neighborhoods and communities without ever feeling a part of them; for many, the church is not the influence it once was. The result is that today we have to cultivate a wholeness that was once thrust upon us; have to pull things together for ourselves in patterns we can deal with.

"An American today sits in a Danish modern chair, with a Picasso on the wall, listening to Mozart on the stereo, reading Dostoevsky—which is fine if he has an inner unity that can compose those disparate elements. Lacking it, he can be fragmented by the things around him. The world we see falling apart on the evening TV news can pull us apart unless our conscious minds and psyches can absorb the chaos around us and make it, and life, into a usable whole.

"Being educated to see the connections between things by an institution that exemplifies wholeness, can be enormously helpful. There is much speculation as to why Princeton alumni are so loyal. I think it's because this is a place they can *comprehend*."

Does Princeton's wholeness get exported in any way to the larger society?

"I think so. I've never thought of 'Princeton in the nation's service' as meaning just that our graduates go to Washington and into politics at other levels. They are useful to society by putting at its service the principles of wholeness they've learned and absorbed here—as professional and business people, as citizens, parents, simply as people dealing with people. They can convey the message that human beings everywhere need to discover, and recognize, and act out of their similarities, their connectedness as human beings, their interrelatedness, if they expect to survive."

Afterword

THOMAS H. KEAN

Encountered at a local hospital benefit, New Jersey
Governor Kean volunteered that he had read *Conversations on the Character of Princeton* and liked it.
Given his reputation as an "education governor," his
background as a teacher, and his having recently accepted
the presidency of Drew University on completion of his
governorship, I wanted to ask *why?*

The opportunity came a few months later when a new
edition of *Conversations* was decided on, and he agreed to
sit for this conversational afterword.

We met at Drumthwacket, official residence of New
Jersey governors, on his last working day as governor. He
had been signing legislation and saying farewells all day;
the state house press corps was gathered in the next room
for a reception; but Kean, at 54, seemed fresh, relaxed,
good-humored, and glad to be talking about a book that
dealt with his first love—teaching.

He said that with this third printing, "*Conversations*
seems on its way to becoming a classic—and deservedly
so."

Why?

Thomas H. Kean—A.B. Princeton (1957), M.A. Columbia Teachers College—taught history and government in secondary schools and at Rutgers
University before entering the state Assembly in 1967. He became speaker in
1974, won the governorship in 1981 by one of the smallest margins in New
Jersey history, and was reelected four years later by the largest. New Jersey
governors can serve only two consecutive terms. Under Kean, the state enacted
44 education reforms. Most important in Kean's opinion are: (1) the alternate
route through which a college graduate can now teach in public schools without
a teachers college degree, and become fully qualified in one year; (2) the
provision whereby the state can now take over and run seriously ailing public
school systems. Drew University is in Madison, New Jersey.

Well, he said, to his knowledge there had never been a book quite like it, "in which dedicated teachers at the top of their professions talk informally about teaching, and about an institution dedicated to teaching.

"It suggests how the character of a university—and by implication any school—affects the performance of its teachers, and how their performance determines the character of the institution."

He pointed out that the book "has already survived some of those who appear in it." One of his Princeton roommates was an English major who "smuggled me into some of Carlos Baker's lectures and preceptorials; Doug Brown, as dean of the faculty, was someone most students knew; and, I was lucky enough to have classes with Alpheus Mason, that great writer on Supreme Court justices. Those three are no longer living, but what they say here about teaching is timeless, and gives the book historical as well as philosophical depth.

"The book increases respect for teaching and adds to the dignity of the profession. It should improve the morale of any teacher reading it, from kindergarten on up. This is important because in a democracy, teachers are the front-line troops. If you don't have democracy, schools are not so important, and good universities not really necessary because the people are told what to do and think. If you *have* democracy, and want to keep it, you need universities where people learn to think for themselves and where the idea of serving the nation is instilled, as it certainly is at Princeton.

"Princeton also, by example, taught me that education is not a matter of passing on knowledge, teachers to students, but of *participation* by students in a back-and-forth process." Echoing William G. Bowen's remark in chapter 2 that "the test of whether one has learned something is whether one can explain it," Kean said students at Princeton and other good schools "learn to teach themselves, and each other. It takes the best of teachers to teach that."

He said he wished every teacher in America could be exposed, through *Conversations,* to the principles and personalities appearing in it, and that the book could be circulated in the new democracies of the world. "It's a profile of a university and the people in it. It takes you to the heart of Princeton, which in many ways could be a model for all teaching institutions from schools to universities."

Finally, he said, "love permeates the book: love of teachers for teaching, for students, and for the material being taught. And love, after all, is what keeps schools and colleges and universities alive and thriving."

We shook hands, and he went out to shake the hands of a hundred or so other reporters.

—W. McC.